NOBODY CARES ABOUT YOUR UNIVERSITY...YET.

The Marketer's Winning Playbook

RITTEN BY **DR. SEAN CARTON** AND **ANDRES ZAPATA** • FOREWORD BY **BOB JOHNSON, PH.D.**

ISBN 978-0-9890136-2-8

Proudly published and printed in
Baltimore, MD, USA.
idfive.com

TABLE OF CONTENTS

ACKNOWLEDGMENTS

A book like this doesn't happen overnight and it doesn't get done without a lot of help. We'd like to acknowledge the expert contribution from our friend and colleague, Anthony D. Paul, for the "Killer Landing Page" and "Research" sections of the book. We'd also like to thank the editorial and subject-matter gut-checking we received from colleagues, including Gigi Boam, Matt McDermott, Michael Warns, Frank Diller and Ira Gewanter.

idfive's Emilee Beeson deserves a sincere level of gratitude for her thoughtful contribution to the cover art concept, illustration, and creative execution. We'd also like thank the entire idfive family for not only making room to push this book through our very busy queue, but also for rallying behind what we know to be a service to the larger higher education marketing community.

Finally, we'd like to thank our clients. This book wouldn't have been possible without your support, collaboration, and belief in the OpenEDU model over the years.

About Bob Johnson, Ph.D.

Bob is president of Bob Johnson Consulting, LLC where he has worked with 85 colleges, universities, and professional associations since 2006 to develop strong marketing communication plans. He is a partner with Gerry McGovern at Customer Carewords, Ltd in Dublin, Ireland.

Bob's popular email newsletter, "Your Higher Education Marketing Newsletter," is sent monthly to 3,500 subscribers around the world. More than 7,300 people around the world follow his "@HighEdMarketing" news on Twitter, and he connects with more than 2,100 people on LinkedIn. He has presented marketing workshops in Australia, Canada, Costa Rica, Denmark, Germany, and the U.S.

FOREWORD

By Bob Johnson, Ph.D.

The State of Higher Education Marketing

This book will help you be a better higher education marketer. After 30 years of higher education marketing, I'm still amazed at both how far we have come and how far we have yet to go.

Yes, we are well past the early years of the AMA Symposium for the Marketing of Higher Education in the late 1980s and early 1990s when attendees were looking for a friendly place where they could use the M-word in public. Back then, most folks could not do that on their own campus. That's no longer the case. "Marketing" is everywhere in higher education, from the highest ranked Ivy League universities to flagship state schools expanding their national reputations; to community colleges promoting their price advantage; to small private sector colleges struggling to stay alive.

Alas, too much of higher education marketing remains overly infatuated with the presumed power of a new logo, a new color on a newly animated website or the quick adoption of the latest online communications app. And, yes, too often we celebrate the adoption of a new brand strategy unrelated to real-world possibilities. Marketing is everywhere, but it is not nearly as successful as it might be.

Three related problems limit the potential for marketing success:

- We are plagued by an excessive devotion to "brand strategy" that pays primary attention to research and creativity. Then we lose focus on the financial resources needed to implement a long-term strategy that achieves substantive results.
- We need more people who strive to be recognized as "tactical marketing experts" and fewer who promote themselves as "brand strategists."
- Research is good. Creative work is good. Strategy is good. But unless a brand strategy is rooted in the reality of what is possible and what is not, it will not work.

Follow the Open Source Higher Education Marketing Model described in the pages here and you are much more likely to create and implement a viable marketing plan that will strengthen your competitive position, improve your enrollment, and enhance your finances.

The OpenEDU Path to Marketing Success

Here are the five best things about the OpenEDU model:

1. **A clear distinction between tactics and strategy**.
   The authors write that "the very first touch" after getting an enrollment lead is critical. Make sure that your marketing tactics—the speed and content of a first email response to a new inquiry, for instance—are solid before you launch a new strategy to spread awareness and increase leads. If your first-response tactics do not work well, you will just frustrate people. Respect for your brand will fall.
   - Email, they note, is not a strategy. But it is an important part of your tactical communications. If it's not done well, respect for enrollment conversions will suffer. "Strategy" will fail.
2. **An emphasis on speed**.
   One thing that has changed dramatically over the past ten years is the expectation that colleges and universities will respond rapidly to potential students from the time of a first inquiry and throughout every stage of a recruitment cycle. Rapid response is key to making a strong first impression on a potential student. If your competitors respond more rapidly than you do, you lose. "Strategy" will fail.
3. **An understanding of brand as a marketing foundation**.
   A marketing plan cannot be stronger than the foundation on which it stands. That might sound simple but too often marketing plans are expected to reach well beyond current brand limitations. Yes, you can change your brand foundation over time. (Think New York University and Northeastern University.) But that takes patience and extended resources. Rather than brand change, most marketing plans are better focused on becoming a stronger competitive force within the parameters set by current brand strength. "Strategy" will succeed.

4. **A goal to set a realistic budget**.

   One of the wisest points presented by the authors is often overlooked: do not set marketing goals and build a marketing plan to achieve them without knowing what the budget will be to support your efforts. A few schools have large marketing budgets—Arizona State University, University of Phoenix, Southern New Hampshire University—but most do not. Force yourself and your president to plan within financial parameters that fit your school's fiscal reality. "Strategy" will succeed.

   - "Goals should be independent of time and budget, right? After all, a goal should encompass what we need to achieve, not what's possible. Wrong." In other words, don't spend big bucks on research and creative for a plan that includes billboards if you can't afford to rent the sites where people will see them. Goals don't buy billboard locations, online ads or staff to handle the new leads you might create.
   - At times it will be best to work with an external marketing agency to provide the resources you might not have on campus. If you do, let the agencies know what your budget is when you send out your RFP. You'll get more realistic proposals and be better able to compare what one agency can deliver compared to another.

5. **The value of secret shopping**.

   You need a marketing plan that helps you compete effectively against other institutions. And that means you need to know what they are doing, from top-level strategy to student recruitment tactics. Become an inquiry at every school that might take the student you'd like to enroll. "Strategy" will benefit.

   - Don't overdo it. Imagine that you had a laser canon on the moon but only three shots to transport competitors to an alternative universe. Which three schools would you pick to transport?
   - And do not, as the authors note, fail to secret shop your own offerings. Comparing yourself against your competitors just might help increase your marketing budget.

That's a quick and incomplete review of what to expect as you read more detail about the OpenEDU pathway to creating and implementing a successful marketing program. Now here are some final notes on marketing and digital challenges.

Marketing Plans and the Digital Era

Marketers are bewitched and bewildered by communication changes in the "digital era." In addition to the five points above, the OpenEDU model helps us understand that while digital communication technology has altered the way marketers connect with people, many of the old principles survive and remain essential to our success.

The most important take-away from the second half of this book is simple: becoming adept at using digital technology has its place. But it is not the single most important thing you must do to survive and thrive today:

"There's one adage about the digital world that we believe to be true: the stuff that works best online is the stuff that can only work online. Online success doesn't come from 'porting' content or business models from one medium to another but rather creating new content and business models to take advantage of the unique properties of digital media."

Another point made in this book illustrates why we should avoid the impulse to quickly adopt new digital phenomena:

- **Teens use desktop and laptop computers**. The authors note the need to understand four related elements in communicating effectively today: audience, intention, context, and device. Apply this approach and you will understand, for instance, why teens do not do everything in the college selection cycle on a smartphone. Ask the students you are recruiting this question: which device do you most often use to access our website? Mobile does not rule the world.

You'll also find a healthy skepticism here about new buzzwords masquerading as startling new marketing innovations. At one point, the authors refer to the "hype" around content marketing. Content marketing is not new. In recent years it has been exploited to justify a deluge of traditional marketing-speak messages, flooding our websites and emails with irrelevant content directed at people who receive… and ignore… it.

- **Effective content marketing is "hard work."** It requires research that identifies the messages people truly want to hear. Effectively done in higher education, that means less on a school's "commitment to academic excellence" and to "educating the whole person" and more on the actual cost of earning a degree and success stories of recent graduates. My personal interest and experience tempts me to say that if you read only one section of this book, go straight to "Killer Landing Pages."
- **Bad landing pages can decimate everything else you do**. If you follow the OpenEDU steps to create a marketing plan but fail to create killer landing pages for the new leads that will come to your website, you have just wasted your time and money. You will wonder why your online advertising or your Search Engine Marketing efforts did not work. You will destroy a fine marketing plan with a poor tactical closing.

Now You Are On Your Own

I haven't attempted to cover the full scope of everything you will find in the OpenEDU marketing model but only tried to whet your appetite to read more. If you do, I have no doubt that you will improve your present marketing efforts and achieve full value for your investment.

If everyone does this, the state of higher education marketing will advance as well.

WHY THIS BOOK?

We started by asking Why write a book in the first place? The answer turned out to be another question: Why hasn't anyone written a book like this before? Higher education—the philosophy, the business model, and the discipline—is in trouble. Big trouble.

Disruptive models in online skills training, corporate education and open-source learning are siphoning off prospective students who traditionally attend colleges and universities. The students who do make it to campus acquire skills that may not be relevant in five years. Faculty and staff scramble to prepare their students for jobs that don't exist yet. Significant student loans, degree farms, and commoditization are contributing to growing concerns about the value of a degree. The outlook is bleak.

Higher education is in a precarious state, and competition is fierce—vicious even—as institutions step on each other to woo a fast-shrinking pool of potential students. Don't think for a second that the new library, recreation center, or residence hall under construction is intended for current students. This competition is, in short, why nobody has written this book, and it's also contributing to the gradual mutation of an industry to a point where some question its viability.

Apocalyptic? Perhaps. But these are issues today's learners wrestle with. We know. We've been asking. And we've been executing successful marketing strategies in this tormented higher education environment, overcoming some of these very barriers to connect with audiences and reinvigorate institutions. Our agency uses a step-by-step playbook to successfully develop and implement marketing, advertising, web, and content strategy initiatives for schools across the United States. This playbook that has served us well. Now we're giving it to you.

We believe that the industry we love will endure, evolve and flourish when higher-ed marketers (and, really, any marketer in a high-stakes environment) are prepared to better connect with existing audiences and inspire new audiences. Consider this book equal parts public service and business preservation. That's why we wrote it.

Let's get started.

INTRODUCTION

Conventional wisdom says everyone who can go to college should go to college. But that falls apart when someone asks why. Is it to train for a job? Learn critical thinking and communication skills? Make lifelong friends? Network with alumni, fraternities or sororities? Find a particular academic field of study worthy of dogged pursuit? Get out of your parents' house?

Traditional colleges and universities offer all of the above. They're all-inclusive destinations ostensibly focused on the transmission of information from those who know to those who don't. But somehow, in the practice of that mission, many graduates face crippling debt and limited job prospects after commencement. Other students drift through campus for a semester or two, find little in the way of inspiration, and move on. Some even manage to mire themselves in debt without getting a degree.

Such students, graduates, and drop-outs are underserved by an industry—yes, higher education is a business—that grew exponentially larger thanks to 20th Century attitudes and policies. Now we're in the 21st Century, questioning the industry's ability to deliver on its promises.

Other industries face similar challenges. Witness the boom and bust cycles of the American automotive, broadcast, and retail industries. They too have struggled to stay relevant in an era marked by dramatic technological, cultural, demographic, and economic changes.

Amid the current state of upheaval, are today's colleges destined to become yet another endangered bastion of brick-and-mortar-based American ingenuity? Maybe. But even within a global "new normal" of constant turmoil, we firmly believe that there are opportunities for our institutions to evolve and thrive.

Our take on higher education—how we got here and, more importantly, how to adapt—is grounded in more than two decades of experience working with colleges and universities. We've collaborated with faculty and staff, navigated internal politics and applied proven strategies to increase our clients' return on investment. We understand your challenges. And we believe in your potential.

Our playbook, the OpenEDU Marketing Strategy Model, is based on proven industry principles and the philosophy of open-source software. Knowledge like this should be free. Take it, share it, and modify it as needed[1].

We hope you'll use these ideas to connect with your audiences more effectively and to inspire new groups to reconsider the value of higher education. It's a commitment borne by care and concern.

Before we dive into the OpenEDU model and its application, however, let's clear up a couple terms that we'll be using a lot throughout this book.

Strategy vs. Tactics

The difference between "strategy" and "tactics" is a persistent classroom stumper that we all struggle to answer at some point. It can be understood in as many ways as there are people thinking about it. Many of the definitions stop just short of being flat-out wrong and land in the nebulous territory of "functionally adequate." Perhaps as a result of this, "strategy" versus "tactics" is misunderstood often enough to warrant clarification.

Here's an easy way to understand the difference:

"Strategy" is where you want to go.

"Tactics" are the roads you can take to get there.

In terms that apply to the OpenEDU Model, "strategy" is usually the "big idea" behind a campaign, why you want to say what you want to say (and to whom), and "tactics" are the different ways to do that.

Let's say you had a waffle shop and wanted to increase revenue. Your *strategy* might be to attract additional business (why) by emphasizing the versatility of your waffles as a food one could eat at any meal (what) to potential new customers (whom). How you get that message out—an email marketing campaign to a list of people in your area who have purchased frozen waffles in the past, a drive-time radio campaign encouraging people to stop by and pick up waffles for dinner, or a giant waffle-shaped balloon floating over your shop touting "Waffles! Hot and ready NOW, good for breakfast, lunch, dinner, or a late-night snack"—are all *tactics* that could serve the strategy you created.

But you're not a waffle shop. If you were, we could probably stop here. Instead, let's take a look at the OpenEDU Model.

THE OPENEDU MARKETING MODEL

Most college or university marketing strategies start life facing a dizzying array of challenges: shifting market forces, paralyzing internal politics, unrealistic timelines, and inadequate funding. In short, even developing a marketing strategy can be risky, and that risk compounds at each stage of follow through. But no matter how much risk you face, chances are the risks associated with inaction are greater. So you still have to move forward.

The good news? The task at hand is not impossible. You just need to manage the risks you face. That's why we developed the "OpenEDU Marketing Model."

The model is based on years of hard work and more than a few hard knocks. We have spent decades testing and tweaking various strategic models. We studied just about everything out there on strategy, branding, and marketing. We even interviewed experts at other marketing firms, ensuring that the OpenEDU Marketing Model is indeed "open."

The result is a synthesis of proven principles and innovative ideas from many brilliant and talented marketers who preceded us. We're standing on the shoulders of giants, and now we want to share the view. We believe that models like this should be free and available because we're all trying to accomplish the same thing: education.

The OpenEDU model is designed to be as simple as possible to understand and implement. While there's a fair amount of complexity in its various modules, the main ideas at the core of the model are designed to be simple: clear, communicable, and succinct.

In this section, we'll introduce the central concepts of the OpenEDU Model. The rest of the book will give you the details you need to put it to work.

The Anatomy of the OpenEDU Model

Think of the OpenEDU model as a cartoon representation of a Classical building. The structure has a foundation, upon which rests three pillars that support a single roof. Simple, right?

The foundation of our structure is your brand platform, the attributes that define and differentiate your institution. It underlies everything you do. Like any foundation, it must be solid, well constructed, and realistically suited to the specific geography of your site.

Resting on this foundation are the three main pillars of the Open EDU model. These pillars represent the three most important areas of tactical focus employed by your marketing plan:

- **Traffic:** The attention you generate from your marketing activities. It can range from brand awareness, to recruitment leads, to open house or event registrations, to website traffic. Most likely, efforts to generate traffic will make up the bulk of your marketing budget.
- **Destination:** The endpoint for your traffic. The destination could be anything from a landing page on the web to a counselor answering the phone in your admissions office. When you generate attention and drive traffic, you want that traffic to go somewhere.
- **Nurture:** The action that occurs when your traffic reaches that destination. Nurturing requires a long-term concerted effort to usher those arrivals toward desired outcomes. Examples include a series of emails designed to move a prospect from interest to enrollment; a set of mailings intended to help parents understand why they should encourage their student to enroll at your institution; or a batch of reminders sent to prospects who expressed an interest in attending your open house. Nurturing is any action that enhances your relationship with your audience.

These three pillars hold up the roof of our structure: the strategy that encompasses all the activities (tactics) that you employ to achieve your desired outcome.

Like any building, ours has to be built to accommodate a number of external forces and influences. Wind, water, gravity, and the people who use the building are "real world" factors. The building's development may also be helped or hindered by a variety of site-specific situational factors such as zoning laws, sustainability goals, or neighborhood aesthetic guidelines. Similarly, construction of our OpenEDU building will accommodate four principal forces and influences that should be recognizable to any marketer. We call these forces inputs.

The four inputs of the OpenEDU model are:

- **Budget:** How much money is allocated to set and execute the strategy?
- **Time:** When is the deadline to implement the strategy?
- **Goal:** What specifically are you trying to accomplish in the short- and long-term?
- **Brand:** How do people feel when they come into contact with your institution?

In the OpenEDU model, the three pillars (marketing plan tactics) are grounded by the foundation (brand platform) and in support of a single, unified roof (strategy). We didn't decide on this conceptualization because we wanted a cute, emoji-ready Greek-temple-looking thingy to represent our model. It's deliberate.

We want you to remember two key points: everything you do must be grounded on your brand platform, and you must have a strong, well-constructed strategy that overlies the tactics you use to implement it.

And we want to emphasize the importance of this with a structure designed so that it would fall apart if you removed any of its elements. We promised a pretty simple model. But the devil's in the details.

As we proceed through the staging of the OpenEDU model, there may come a time when you think, "Well, that's not how I would go about building a three-pillared Greek-temple-looking thingy." Please bear in mind that this is a visual analogy for a successful marketing plan. We're not building an actual Greek temple.

Start with Some Internal Assessments

The OpenEDU Model will guide you through a massive decision tree. The following checklist ensures that you ask the right questions for each module, keeping you on the right path toward a killer strategic marketing plan.

Inputs

1. **Budget**
   - How much was approved for the current fiscal year?
   - How much has been spent, and what is committed for the rest of the year?
   - How much is in the budget for the next fiscal year?
   - Are there good internal resources available for graphic design, programming, copywriting, social media, videography, public relations, or photography?
   - Are there any budget items scheduled for other things (social media, web development, marketing redesigns, etc.) that you can roll into this effort?
   - Will there be enough money to do a sustained push? Or will there only be enough to stagger a showing?
2. **Time**
   - When is the next recruitment cycle in full swing?
   - When is the campaign expected to launch?
   - When do you expect to measure results?
   - When will admissions be ready to take on an influx of inquiries?
   - When will the school be staffed to take on the new students?
   - Are there any national or religious holidays when you should push or pause marketing?
3. **Goal**
   - What, specifically, needs to be accomplished in the short term?
   - Are there any sub-goals to consider?
   - How will you measure success?

4. Brand(ing)

- What is the current brand platform?
- What are the core brand attributes?
- What are the extended brand attributes?
- What graphic, or other media-based elements, are used to express your brand?
- Is there a tagline?
- How will you deal with sub-brands (e.g., well-known schools/colleges within your institution)?
- How much awareness do your target audiences have about your brand?
- How is your brand perceived in the outside world?
- What are people saying about your institution on social media?

Pillars

1. Traffic

- Are there events, such as open houses, that people can attend?
- Are there landing pages for web traffic?
- What's the geography to cover with the advertising/outreach effort?
- Which traffic sources have shown promise in the past?
- Which traffic sources have bombed in the past?
- How much traffic is needed to achieve the desired lead generation at 5% conversion? (I.e., where 5 out of every 100 people say, "Sure, tell me more.")

2. Destination

- Is the destination a landing page or a microsite?
- Has the destination been optimized for copy, design, and transaction?
- Is the destination responsive for mobile and tablet users?
- Have all the tracking codes been added to the destination?

- Are the calls to action jumping off the page?
- Have you tested the collection form?
- Does it usher data effectively into the CRM?
- Is the destination a location/event?
- Has the event's location been clearly marked from the street? (I.e., can people see it when they walk / drive by?)
- Have enough people been trained to help "mine" the prospects?
- Is there swag that prospects can take with them?
- Have all representatives been trained to:
    - Use the right language and "asks"?
    - Overcome objections?
    - Handle a situation when they get stuck?

3. Nurture

- What is the ultimate goal? Application? Enrollment? Reconsidering your institution if they've been accepted but have yet to enroll?
- What defines a "lead"?
- How much information do you need to collect to consider a lead "captured"?
- Among different audience segments, what is the very first touch they will receive after they are a "lead"?
- How soon after they become a lead will that first touch occur?
- Can you integrate multiple touch points into your flow (e.g., text messaging, telephone calls, in-person visits, etc.)?
- What are some logical communication flows that can be segmented by audience, season, or place in the recruitment cycle?
- Do you have the resources (and the flexibility) to test different messaging, timing, or other attributes of your campaign?
- Can you effectively ingest the communication flows into a CRM?
- Will the communication flows track open rates and click-through rates?

Case Study: The OpenEDU Model in Action

Probably the best way to understand how the OpenEDU model works is to see it in action.

A business school at a major East Coast university hired idfive after its fifth academic year. Just like almost every school, they were in search of enrollments. But the need was particularly acute because the program was young and relatively unproven. Even though they had a major university brand behind them, this was a new frontier: the high-stakes, highly competitive world of graduate business education. They needed to gain a foothold. Fast.

We began our engagement by working to understand their situation—and the general condition of graduate business education—as thoroughly as possible. We conducted discussion groups with faculty, students, staff, and prospects and triangulated the feedback with third-party environmental research to develop a clear picture of the school's brand and value proposition. We also worked hard to develop a better understanding of audience segmentation. This was no small task considering that they offered programs appealing to local, regional and international audiences.

This research led us to the development of the first piece of the OpenEDU puzzle: the brand platform. We recognized the global nature of the school along with the shared values of the institution, values that put people first. It was a strong differentiator—businesses schools aren't exactly known for caring. And it rang true due to the university's record of distinction in the health professions and sciences.

Once we had a solid foundation to work with, we developed a strategy that emphasized structured flexibility and focused primarily on digital media. Digital is so responsive and flexible, we were able to use the data we gathered from our marketing efforts to measure and fine-tune our approach as close to real-time as possible.

Three pillars supported this strategy. Targeted online display advertising and paid search drove traffic to a destination of program-specific landing pages; and an interactive program finder helped guide prospective students to the programs that best fit their needs. (It also helped us capture additional data about prospect interests.)

After we captured the data, we nurtured the relationship with a series of personalized emails and mailings. Whether a prospect requested information or wanted to attend an open house, we worked closely with Admissions to develop a program that helped keep that person engaged over the long, decision-making period that's typical of graduate school. We gradually moved them to apply and enroll.

Of course, we operated under a number of constraints, not the least of which was our promise to be held accountable for stewardship of the budget. This required regular feedback about results and close collaboration with our in-house partners in making decisions about how to fine-tune the program for greatest response. We were also under a fair amount of time pressure since the client needed to drive enrollments up as soon as possible.

Our joint goal was to focus on response and conversion first and worry about building brand awareness over time as the program progressed. Finally, while we had the brand equity of a world-class university working in our favor, we knew that execution needed to be flawless in order to deliver a brand experience that matched the expectations of the target audiences.

The result? During the first five years, leads increased 903% and enrollments went up 83.14%. Meanwhile, the budget remained relatively flat. We had captured so much data during the program that we were also able to go back and analyze the direct impact our marketing efforts had on enrollments. The results were clear: our plan worked.

And that wasn't even the best news. Prior to working with us, the business school's cost-per-lead was in the hundreds of dollars. Our most recent work has gotten that cost-per-lead down to $46 per highly qualified prospect.

By focusing on data, developing a plan based on the OpenEDU model, and understanding the constraints of time, budget, goals, and brand, we helped this business school take wing and fly.

Now that you understand the basics of the OpenEDU model and have spent some time getting a better idea of how the model can help you shape the tactical elements of your marketing plan, let's take a step back and look at what holds it all together: strategy.

PREPARING THE GROUND

PART 1: INTERNAL ASSESSMENT

The OpenEDU model likens marketing plans to a building. We believe the metaphor merits belaboring since people often treat marketing like an ethereal, even mystical, process that isn't worthy of the same care as a physical construction. Since the consequences of failure can be dire in either case, let's revisit the analogy.

Building a quality structure requires more than just choosing a plan and selecting materials. Before any of that begins, you must select a suitable location and prepare the ground to properly ensure stability of the eventual construction. Marketing plans aren't any different: to succeed they must incorporate a thorough survey of the "lay of the land."

This means conducting a review of all of the potential aspects of your eventual campaign that you may not be able to control. We mentioned four inputs earlier, and we'll be taking a look at those more in depth later. For now, we're looking at the ground we're building on. Ground as in dirt. As in the nitty gritty.

Before constructing your foundational brand platform, overarching strategy, and supportive tactical pillars, you must conduct two areas of research to "prepare the ground"— internal and external. We address this first because in our work we have found it best to understand as much as possible before proceeding.

Internal Assessment: Yes, You Have To

To develop and execute a successful marketing strategy, it's vital that you fully comprehend the marketing problem that your marketing program is supposed to fix. And understanding your marketing problem in its entirety isn't easy. You have to know your organization and what motivates people inside the organization to seek out more powerful marketing tactics. You need to understand how your internal capacities and resources can (or can't) support the logistics of a campaign. You need to know what success looks like and have the ability to identify failure so that you can avoid it. And, even scarier, you will eventually have to use this understanding to react and make decisions about how to proceed.

The hardest part of developing and executing successful strategy is looking at yourself and asking the hard questions. Nobody likes to do this in their lives outside of work, and they certainly don't like doing it when surrounded by their colleagues.

Why? Because asking questions like "why are we doing this?" requires people to go out on a limb and declare to the world that they know the answer to a very complicated question. But, as we've seen in many of the strategic planning sessions we've facilitated, many people are afraid to go out on that limb, especially if they have to take an unpopular position or face (what they may see as) unnecessary scrutiny. Unfortunately, in most cases, people tend to shy away from the great, but risky, ideas. Instead, they trade on safe, mediocre concepts. The resulting strategy is often a muddled mess that can't prompt change because it won't risk change.

On the other hand, while people are often reticent to offer positive solutions to problems, they're often ready to share their opinions when it comes to more, shall we say, *negative* options. While it's scary to answer the question "what should we do?" it's a lot less frightening to respond to the question "what *shouldn't* we do?"

If you want to test how this works, use the negative approach the next time you're standing around with your colleagues trying to decide where to go for lunch. Unless you work somewhere where only one choice exists, deciding where to go can be a nightmare because nobody wants to step on anyone else's toes (or expose themselves to criticism) by suggesting a destination. Eventually, one person, driven nearly mad by hunger and frustration, declares a choice. Everyone follows suit, glad to be done with the polite (and highly irritating) group indecision.

> **THE RESULTING STRATEGY IS OFTEN A MUDDLED MESS THAT CAN'T PROMPT CHANGE BECAUSE IT WON'T RISK CHANGE.**

If, however, instead of asking for suggestions on where to go, you ask for suggestions where not to go, you face a very different dynamic. Everyone will make their preferences known by listing the places where they don't want to go. In most cases, there are no objections to the very limited number of choices that are left. Bingo! Decision made!

Eliminating what's not going to work often leads you to what will work. As Sherlock Holmes said in *The Sign of the Four*, "How often have I said to you that when you have eliminated the impossible, whatever remains, however improbable, must be the truth?"

Elementary, dear reader! Keep this approach in mind while undergoing the following internal assessment.

The Nine Key Questions

While admissions, marketing, and students services are often divided into silos on campus—working with different priorities, leadership, and budgets—together they are responsible for total tuition revenue. That means all of the parties will need to share some semblance of a unified vision and approach to succeed. But before you can get where you want to go, you have to know where you are.

Start by inviting every stakeholder to answer the following questions. These prompts are designed to develop consensus about what problems exist, why, and how you can get a preliminary glimpse into which brand platform, strategy, and tactics might be best suited to the reality of the institution.

You may make people uncomfortable during the process. That's great. When you're probing assumptions and evaluating existing systems, you can't take anything for granted. Just remember that you're challenging constraints—not the people bound to them.

If you and your colleagues are honest and thorough in this phase, you will eventually be able to create a shared vision and a sound, defensible plan for making it happen. So be brave! It's worth it.

YOU MAY MAKE PEOPLE UNCOMFORTABLE DURING THE PROCESS. THAT'S GREAT.

1. **What happens if we do nothing?**
   This should be the first question asked at any meeting—or at least before launching any new initiative. It forces you to confront reality based on current conditions and trends. If enrollments are down, and the pool of prospective students is shrinking, it won't be hard to see what the future holds by maintaining the status quo.

2. **What are we trying to accomplish?** In the proverb of the blind men and the elephant, a group of people identifies the animal based on the part they touch: a trunk is a snake, a leg is a tree, etc. It's subjective, incomplete and, ultimately, an inexact approach.

   Whenever we tackle a problem, we see it through the lens of our own experience. Marketing or communications people may think of recruitment as brand awareness. Admissions folks might consider contact with prospects. Student affairs departments might focus on campus life. And faculty members may pay attention to the pedagogical experience.

   It's in our nature to do this, but that tendency can fuel arguments about institutional programs and political turf. Instead, stick to specific, measurable answers.

   If you're inclined to "raise awareness," ask how to measure future brand awareness of your institution against recognition in your current market. If the goal is to "increase enrollment," request specifics: Why do you need to increase enrollment? By how much? Over what period?

   These details make it easier to move from fuzzy generalities to measurable, actionable goals. Then the full elephant comes into focus. Finally, remember there's no right answer to any of these questions.

THE PROGRAM FINDER

How do you help prospective graduate students navigate the huge range of options available to them at a large public institution?

One client, a land grant university, offered almost every path, including law, medicine, social work, nursing and even thanatology. Each of the graduate schools was relatively independent, housing separate admissions offices and creating distinct recruitment marketing campaigns. It was a big, complex place that could intimidate someone interested in the wide range of possible professions.

The university asked us to create a strategy to guide prospects to the programs they needed while also helping to develop leads for their recruitment efforts. We created the Program Finder, an interactive tool that asks visitors to identify their needs and educational interests and then returns a matrix of programs based on the prospect's criteria.

The Program Finder makes it easier for prospects to find what they want and helps the graduate school gather information about prospects based on their answers. The result is a win for prospects and the institution, providing valuable insights to both groups.

3. **What does success look like?**
By defining success as explicitly as possible, you can set initial benchmarks and ongoing milestones. Plus, you can explain why the measures you're using are important. Let's say your answer to Question #2 was, "Increase enrollment by 20% over five years." Great. Now define exactly how you want that to happen: What are current enrollments? How and when will an increase occur? Is it acceptable if enrollments are flat for four years, but you hit your goal in Year Five? Is it realistic to expect an annual increase of 4%? Or do you need to ramp up gradually? Why? Then think about the implications of your success: How will reaching this goal affect the institution? Do you have the capacity to absorb these new students? If not, what will have to happen to support them?

BY DEFINING SUCCESS AS EXPLICITLY AS POSSIBLE, YOU CAN SET INITIAL BENCHMARKS AND ONGOING MILESTONES.

Based on what you know about your current pool of prospective students, will your institution have to lower admissions standards to reach that goal? If so, how will that impact your brand? Remember, an incomplete answer is better than no answer at all. After all, no plan ever survives contact with reality.

4. **What resources do we have available?**
Resources aren't limited to money in the budget. We've seen schools fail by not anticipating that increased spending on recruitment marketing will affect the staff charged with responding to new leads. The marketing budget might be available to push the number of leads generated through the roof, but when they could go straight into an Admissions office black hole, languishing in a database of prospects to be contacted "some day," then yield will drop. Then everyone wonders why the spiffy new advertising campaign—and bigger budget—didn't produce the desired results.

Even worse, prospects that haven't received the information they requested now have a negative perception of the institution. And that's an attitude they may be happy to share with peers on social networks. Also, factor in institutional resources, such as hardware, software and physical space. If your plan requires a new database, phone system, or access to additional facilities, can you get these resources when you need them? The fourth question is especially tricky if you're dependent upon other departments. If you don't have a guarantee that resources will be available when you need them, don't count them as "available" in your strategic plan.

5. **Who are we trying to reach?**
   Start with defining your audiences in a classic way by examining factors such as demographics, geography, and level of academic achievement. Once you get these factors down, you can start moving into more complex territory, including psychographic and sociological dimensions. Then, look at how context comes into play: Are there situational aspects that might impact who is more or less likely to choose your institution? Does a specific moment in the decision-making process affect how you reach out to your intended audience? Could external factors that don't fit into typical audience definitions make your target audience more or less appropriate for the new campaign? Are there any social, cultural, or economic trends that make your institution more or less attractive to a particular group? Are there any technological trends that impact these audiences and how you reach them? Finally, consider defining the "customer journeys" that lead to your institution.

   Discovery: Why might your audience consider continuing their education? What kinds of trends or changes influence that decision? If they've decided, what's the next step? Do they ask friends and family? Do they consult with business colleagues? Do they just Google it? If so, what keywords might they use? How long do they take to build their list of potential institutions? How much time does it take before acting on that list and reaching out for more information? What type of information do they need, and when do they need it?

   Decision: Once they have the information, which factors are most or least important to them? At what point do they begin the application process? Which factors influence their decision to enroll in one institution over another?

Commitment: What might make them reject an acceptance offer? What would help change that decision? How do we minimize "melt"? Everyone exists in a social network, and people within that network exert different kinds of influence during your prospect's journey. Identifying this sphere of influence is as important as knowing your target audiences—especially when thinking about parents of traditional undergraduates or families of continuing-ed students. For example, an accelerated weekend program might make a lot of sense in theory, but it may not be very attractive to someone with children. In that case, prospects' significant others might be just as—if not more—important to reach as the prospects themselves.

6. **Why them?**
   More than typical "marketing" stuff like media and creative choices, this requires understanding how your effort affects your institution. Break free from "conventional wisdom." It's easy to get into a rut, going after the same prospective student pool every year—especially when it produces results. But what if your yields start to decline? Maybe it's time to look at different prospect groups to see how well they align with institutional priorities. It might require an examination of admissions standards or changes in demographic trends that affect your traditional pool. Or maybe you need to look for opportunities in groups traditionally underserved by your institution. The possibilities are endless, but no matter which groups you decide to pursue, you need to be able to answer why you're going after them and how your institution is a qualified candidate for their academic and professional plans.

7. **If we do this, what are we going to do less of?**
   In our experience, no one has an unlimited budget. (If you do, please contact us immediately). A new project often means doing less of something else. And this discussion often has staffing implications. Re-assigning or eliminating personnel—especially if you're going to replace them with new people that bring a different skill set—is never easy, particularly at a college or university. Take a hard look at places where you might duplicate efforts, or would do so if you pursued a new strategy. If it happens, you may be able to get by—or even

free up additional resources—by shifting resource allocations. Next, examine your various initiatives by asking some hard questions: Why are you doing what you're doing? What are you (specifically) trying to accomplish? Is the initiative succeeding? If not, or if you don't know why because you can't measure performance, consider ending the initiative to do something new. It may seem risky, but it's probably worse to continue to waste resources.

8. **Which internal processes or politics will have an impact on what we're trying to do?**
"Politics" and "processes" are often inextricably linked. Usually, things are done the way they are done because someone wants them done that way. The *safe* thing to do is to accept them and deal with the situation. The *right* thing to do is to take a hard look at what's going on and why. You may find that you can't change what's going on. That's OK: at least you've identified the problem. However, sometimes you *can* do something, especially if what's happening is under your direct area of responsibility. The key is to understand what's going on and which outcomes it's generating.

   One of the most common ways politics and processes collide is when someone's been in a position long enough to serve as the "institutional memory." They are black boxes, taking inputs and producing outputs without anyone having any idea what they're actually doing to make necessary decisions. And while it may have worked at one time, in practice, many of these people are bottlenecks or obstructions to progress. It's vital to your strategic planning to be honest about what impact these people, or units, are going to have on your efforts.

If Admissions routinely ignores your requests for information about how and when they follow up on leads that you provide, you need to consider this in your planning and not count on receiving information from them. If graduate program recruitment happens at the department or program level, you are dependent upon the department chair or program director to follow up with prospects *and* provide you with some indication of how well your graduate recruitment initiatives are going. If they're not doing either one, consider alternative methods to accomplish your goal. For example, if your information request forms go directly to the program director, send a copy to your office as well, so you have some of the information you need. Also, ask friends and family to "secret shop" for you by sending in requests for information and then reporting to you on what they receive. It provides insight into the players, politics, and processes that are vital to your strategy.

9. **Who's going to be in charge?**
   Understanding roles and responsibilities should be obvious, but it rarely is. If the person responsible for implementing your strategy isn't capable of making the decisions required to keep it on track—or if you can't figure out whom that person should be—your strategy is doomed to failure. While the unfortunate truth may be that you can't do anything to change the situation, knowing who is ostensibly in charge will help you craft an executable strategy realistically designed to either distribute responsibility or alleviate the need for too much intervention.

On the other hand, you may need to account for someone who either doesn't agree with your strategy or has a competing (but unspoken) strategy. Again, you may not be able to do anything about it, but you can account for its effect, positive or negative, on what you're trying to accomplish.

UNDERSTANDING ROLES AND RESPONSIBILITIES SHOULD BE OBVIOUS, BUT IT RARELY IS.

As you work through these nine questions, remember that you and your team can't control every factor. Mitigate risk by answering each question as honestly and comprehensively as possible. Then revisit them throughout the life of your project to keep everyone on the same page.

Once your team shares a common vision—or as close to one as you can muster—you're ready to gather information about the external factors facing you.

Case Study: Understanding Who You Are

It was a fun assignment: redesign the website of a private, faith-based, selective small college located in the southwestern U.S. We knew that doing the right thing would depend on us understanding the institution and its audiences in as much depth as possible.

We began with a multi-day visit to the campus where our plan was to talk to as many people as possible and, just as importantly, to experience the school for ourselves. What did it feel like to be on campus? What was it like to interact with the faculty, staff, and students? What set the institution apart? Why did people decide to attend the school?

One of the most lasting images—and the one that helped us understand the people of the institution better than almost anything else—was the wall of backpacks lining the entrance to the cafeteria. The backpacks, hanging from hooks and sitting on the floor, were unattended. They awaited their owners to retrieve them before going back to class.

It was a small detail, but these backpacks represented the perfect distillation of the sense of trust, openness, and community that permeated the campus.

Even though many people on the outside perceived the school to be a somewhat conservative institution, the campus prided itself on intellectual inquiry and rigorous academics. It was founded on a "great books" model with a core curriculum shared by all undergraduates, an approach that led to a level of community and shared purpose that we'd rarely seen anywhere else. Thanks to this sense of community, the faculty, students, staff, and administration were unified in their commitment to intellectual inquiry, rigorous thought, and a mission to serve the world.

We used these brand attributes in a website design focused on communicating the same sense of joy, wonder, and, to be honest, surprise that we experienced on campus. And it taught us that insight sometimes comes from unexpected places.

PART II: EXTERNAL (AUDIENCE) ASSESSMENT

You have to know your audience as well as their motivations. Today's college students are shaped by ever-changing and often elusive market, social, and technological forces. Of these, however, technology has had the most profound impact on how people consume media, and how, what and when they act on it.

The most influential technological innovations often become invisible. From human flight to smartphones, we tend to follow a standard pattern for facilitating and adapting to change: Marvel at the breakthrough. Adjust our lives to accommodate it. Take it for granted. Complain when it fails.

As innovations merge with daily life, however, they continue to disrupt our culture. The Internet has forced numerous industries—music, movies, etc.—to evolve for survival. Digital technology has freed content from its containers, altering how and when people choose to engage. And those changes have had significant implications for higher education as well.

Before the printing press, the church was the gatekeeper of most information. Prior to the Golden Age of Google, colleges and universities were the de facto gatekeepers of information. Research findings, scholarly journals and conference proceedings sat on library shelves. Lectures occurred in a shared physical space at a designated time. Alumni reconnected during return visits to campus. Today most of this information is freely available to anyone with an Internet connection.

Screen Time

In the early days of the Web, cyber pundits talked about "convergence," the idea that the Web would, at some point, merge all the content we consume into one screen. Instead, during the past decade, a variety of smaller screens arrived to create a more portable, personal experience. In fact, the idea of the family gathering together around one screen seems as anachronistic as those images of families sitting by the radio for FDR's "fireside chats" or standing around a piano for a sing-along. If we're not watching content fed to us in real time—sports and breaking news, for the most part—we're watching it individually on our own screens. For the first time in human history, the home no longer has a literal or figurative "hearth."

Today, it's common to use multiple devices simultaneously. We glide between tabs, windows, and screens. Cameras document personal experiences. Social media broadcasts thoughts from any environment. "Sharing economy" services, such as Airbnb and Uber, match needs to available resources by location. And we create our own realities mediated through the devices we carry and the experiences we choose to have through them.

> **FOR THE FIRST TIME IN HUMAN HISTORY, THE HOME NO LONGER HAS A LITERAL OR FIGURATIVE "HEARTH."**

We use digital space to automate, moderate, and facilitate our interactions with others. We're never truly alone when the digital bond spans space and time, reaching out across Facebook, Twitter, Instagram, Snapchat, and other apps to construct our realities and our relationships. The virtual monsters in *Pokemon Go* are just as real as the people we edit with our Instagram filters. Use these applications enough and we start to think of these applications as natural extensions of our lives in the Digital Age.

In the physical world, context is based on four dimensions: width (x), height (y), depth (z) and time (t). It's the foundation for where and when we live. But that's changing in the multi-screen universe.

Our new environment requires four different dimensions: *audience* (who), *intention* (why), *context* (where or when) and *device* (what). Understanding how the audiences we're trying to reach exist in these new digital dimensions is the key to crafting effective messaging and anticipating audience needs.

Personas Work

If we're going to connect to our "audience segments," we need to see them not as numbers or abstract concepts but as human beings. Designers, usability experts, and developers use personas to humanize our conception, testing ideas, approaches, designs, products and services.

Personas aren't real people. Instead, they're stand-ins, representing how we think real people might act based on how we define them and what they might think about what we're selling. They might not be "real," but their situations, motivations, and actions are... at least in the aggregate.

You can use personas to map the wants and needs of real audiences to your institution's offerings. For example, if you offer an undergraduate program and three graduate programs, you could create four personas to represent the people who are interested in those programs. As you dive into the project, however, you may find that you'll need to create additional personas to capture the finer distinctions between the audiences you're trying to represent.

Creating Personas

To create a persona of a prospective student, ask yourself the following questions while trying to imagine how your target audiences might answer them:

- Why do you want to earn this degree?
- How do you think this degree will impact your life?
- Who, if anyone, will help you make this decision?
- What are your apprehensions?
- How does who you are (age, gender, income, etc.) impact your decision?
- How does your physical location affect your decision?
- What is your timeline to make a decision?

Personas don't have to be complicated or time-consuming to create. If they ring true as reasonable facsimiles of the people you're trying to communicate with, they're probably good enough. If you want to make them more "real" for your team, give the personas a name and use stock photography to represent their physical presence. Either way, a cursory approach to defining each audience will help you craft meaningful marketing decisions.

As you create your personas, remember to be honest. You can't be all things to all people. Colleges and universities face retention issues when they try to sell someone on false promises. Focus on prospects that your institution can handle from an operational, academic and logistical perspective. You're invoking people who can use existing services rather than creating new services that might appeal to ideal candidates. Don't try to re-create the world.

Hearts, Minds, Screens

Age, socioeconomic status, gender, and ethnicity are big factors when it comes to defining when and how people engage with their screens. And smartphones are increasingly the method of choice for many when interacting with the world, especially for "traditional" college-bound prospects.

Let's say we want to reach high school students, ages 16 to 18, who are browsing college options. Those two data points—*16-18-year-olds looking at colleges*—give us the "who" and "why" we need to begin the construction of useful personas. The next step is to infer context and the device (or devices) they might use in their search.

If your prospect lives at home, she may use a laptop or desktop to research and organize large amounts of information. Even so, when she's interacting with her friends on social media and discussing college possibilities she may use a smartphone.

That device recognition helps you to craft your message and optimize it for various platforms. A device with a large screen and a lot of computing power gives us the luxury to share immersive content, such as a high-definition video, or a graphically intense interactive experience, including virtual tours. On the other hand, when your prospective student is using a smartphone you'll need to offer navigational and contextual information geared to a small screen.

The key to dealing with these situations is an understanding of how context changes information needs and behaviors. But it's not just the technology that's different: the situations are probably different as well. Desktop and laptop machines are far better suited for complex searches, content creation, and collating vast amounts of information and typically used in a fixed location for longer periods of time. You can probably engage them with in-depth content and expect that they're willing to learn more general information about your institution.

Smartphones—and, to some extent, tablets—are more suited to directed, short-term information browsing that's often triggered by a need dictated by their physical situation. The devices are used for shorter amounts of time and most frequently accessed when the user is "on the go" from one location to another. They're probably looking for shorter and more focused information that answers a specific question, often a question that has to do with where they are at any given time.

Design Experience

Today's web illustrates the evolution of marketing and brand experience. Before the iPhone arrived, designers conceptualized most websites in the same way they thought about annual reports. The content was organized logically, often in a linear sequence. Screen layouts were optimized to make it easier to read long-form content. More content required? Just repeat the same formula.

New screen sizes required new rules. Responsive design—websites that resize themselves to match the size of the viewing screen—was a critical step in making sure that various devices could access valuable content. But what if there's no screen?

As we continue to enter the "Internet of Things" era—where fitness bands track steps and vital signs, augmented reality devices enhance the "real world," and social apps communicate to us on the go—we need to start thinking beyond the look of a web page. It's necessary to consider how we can express an institution's core values and brand experience in any medium and on any device, even if that device has no screen.

Probably the best way to imagine how to communicate in the future is to look at brands that have managed to transform their representation from graphic, audible, and interactive digital elements to become "brand experiences" that are identifiable anywhere they're encountered. Disney is one of the most accessible examples of brand transformation, using iconic elements to create an emotional bond that reinforces the brand even without specific "messaging" or graphic elements. When we encounter a Disney experience, we know it, even if we can't hear or see branded content, such as the classic silhouette of Mickey Mouse's head or the tagline, "The happiest place on earth."

If your school is doing its job well, alumni, faculty, and students may have similar feelings about your institution. There's something special that happens when they encounter your institution anywhere. If you want to be able to communicate that experience, you need to ask yourself: What does it look like? How does it feel? When do you promote it? Can you share that connection with a prospective student or a potential donor?

Your websites and landing pages are part of the experience. They are the bridge that connects digital and interactive elements online to how students and prospects feel when they enter lobbies of your buildings; how they experience campus signage when they're trying to find a particular building; how they feel when they end a call with an admissions counselor; or even when an email reminder helps them do something important that they may have forgotten otherwise. If they feel like they're communicating with your brand even when they don't realize it, then you have succeeded.

The long-term goal of all of this is to create a deep, emotional bond that feels natural and personal. You want engagement, not events.

Design Killer Landing Pages and Microsites

If you want to improve your understanding of how to connect at a minimal cost, consider building landing pages or microsites that fulfill a particular need or target a subset of your audience. They provide a place to test innovative approaches to attract and engage prospects.

Today every web page on your site is a potential starting point in a prospect's journey. Search, social sharing, and traditional marketing materials drive traffic to target different areas. If you can't anticipate a person's intent, context, and device, you're at risk of making a bad first impression.

"Engagement" is more than a headline or an interactive experience that keeps someone on a page for a longer-than-usual time. If you want to engage your visitors, you've got to be prepared to ask, listen, and personalize content for your visitors. Keep the following guidelines in mind as you create a killer landing page or microsite:

1. **Be Everything for Someone**
   Present and amplify core messaging, tasks, and calls to action. What does this persona want to see and do to complete a transaction? If you've got it, great. Don't water things down with secondary requirements or content that appeases an internal stakeholder more than it appeals to a prospect.

2. **Create Accessible, Usable, Appropriate Content**
   Understand how the page relates to a step in the user journey/decision-making process. Lean on a prospect's existing knowledge of your institution so you can emphasize the next steps without being redundant.
3. **Personalize Forms**
   Customer Relationship Management tables prioritize contact information over personal interests. It's more than likely that your intended audience thinks about it in reverse. Imagine having a conversation with prospects. Ask about their interests and passions, then request contact information.
4. **Trim Required Fields**
   What is the least amount of information you need to create a conversion? Is it a name and an email address? Then why require a phone number, date of birth, or zip code? Fewer requirements will yield more conversions.
5. **Design for the Device**
   Landing pages need to be responsive and functional on the devices and networks that prospects use. Think about real-world usage and validate designs by testing with those environments and constraints.
6. **Use the Reader's Voice While Maintaining Brand Authority**
   Higher education needs to sound smart and personable. You're not writing research papers—or Hallmark cards. You're engaging human beings; don't be afraid to write like one.
7. **Use Action Verbs**
   Headlines should allow a reader to envision the next step: "Browse Our Programs"; "Join Our Newsletter"; "Follow Us on Twitter." (If you don't think it helps, "Read This Numbered List Again.")
8. **Define a Clear Call to Action—and Support It**
   Make sure your users know what you want them to do: State the purpose of your landing page. Provide a button with a clear call-to-action. Add a call-to-action as an in-context text link, either within or at the end of a paragraph. Run a usability test. Know that all of the content leads to and persuades the desired action.

9. **Test, Measure, Revise**
   If you're torn between two techniques, try both. It is easier to launch two landing pages rather than one, and you can run an A/B test. Track conversions for a brief period, then select the better performing option as the destination for every visitor. Everything's open for testing, including button labels, colors, and the order of content. Use your data to resolve internal debates.

A successful landing page empowers a prospect and yields results. Your greatest challenge may be advocating for limited content that achieves its sole purpose. Data are your best friend when it comes to determining what works well in every step of your prospect's journey. Knowing what type of data to collect is as important as knowing what to do with it. And if you want to gather data, you're going to have to be prepared to do some research.

Case Study: Content Strategy Discovery

One constant we've recognized over the years is that most website redevelopment projects run into trouble when it comes to one element: content. Everything else—design, development, production—might go on without a hitch, but as soon as it's time to "feed the beast" and put content into the site, it's easy for things to go sideways quickly.

To be honest, content is usually a problem for established websites. And for good reason: most institutions aren't structured to be publishers. Even if a school has a division dedicated to publishing, the people hired for most administrative tasks didn't get their jobs because of their ability to publish content. And when they're charged with creating content, it's usually a task for "when they have time." Which they don't.

However, if you look at the whole idea of producing content at your institution, people who aren't considered content experts have been tasked with producing content for a long time. Considering the state of most hallway bulletin boards and quad kiosks we see at our partner schools, producing flyers, memos, or other paper-based publications doesn't seem to be a problem. The issue is publishing information to the web.

This was the situation we found ourselves in when we were hired by a major health sciences campus in the South. While the campus certainly didn't suffer from a lack of communication, making the transition to the web had been tough. Like many schools, this one had decided that the web was "technology" and technology stuff belonged in the IT department.

A small web team, consisting of less than ten hard-working folks in the Information Technology department, managed tens of thousands of web pages. They worked valiantly to keep the content flood at bay. With a few exceptions—one school on the campus seemed to have a somewhat functional content-publishing structure—everything that had to go on the website had to flow through these folks.

While this may have been a workable approach a decade ago, it became completely untenable. Few on campus were happy, and nobody knew what to do. That's when they called us.

We knew that in order to solve their problem we had to learn everything we could about how content was created, trafficked, and published on their website. We had to understand what kinds of expectations were in place, how the various professional schools on the campus dealt with content destined for the web, and how the process had worked up until the point we arrived.

In order to discover what we needed to know, we talked to people…lots of people. Over the course of two days, we interviewed everyone responsible for web content in every school on campus, as well as those in the central administration who published content for all. We interviewed senior leadership in order to discover their priorities and to uncover how web content fit into the larger campus strategic direction.

In addition to conducting interviews, we also led the current web team and content creators through a series of workshops. We helped uncover their mental models for content creation so they could understand the impact of their content on the campus website.

In the end, we collaborated with the web team to develop a new plan of action and a process that would help distribute content management throughout the entire institution. After we identified that this task was an additional responsibility for most content creators, we knew education would be a big part of our plan. If people didn't know what to do, the important work wouldn't get done.

At the end of the engagement, we delivered three things that came directly from our research into content management practices:

- recommendations for a structure that would support distributed sustainable content management;
- recommendations for additional personnel to support the new way of distributing content responsibilities; and
- educational materials delivered as a "how to write for the web" Wiki that could serve as the foundation for the initial changes they had to make and an ongoing resource designed to support long-term change.

Research

You may recognize this scene as an all-too-common design presentation: pitch, change, pitch again. It continues as a series of increasingly frustrating meetings that seem to go on forever. Everyone is unhappy. No one agrees on an acceptable design. Sadly, the entire relationship ends in disaster.

We call this "Design Battleship." Just like the board game where players take turns calling out different coordinates to try to "hit" the opposing player's ships, it can be maddening to aim for a target you can't see. The Battleship board is a 10-by-10 grid; the killing fields of Design Battleship can go on forever.

There are lots of causes for Design Battleship, but we've found that the main reason is subjective criteria. Anything that's open to an opinion has the potential to be misinterpreted and misunderstood. If you're lucky, tastes eventually align, and a design is chosen. If not, things can go south quickly.

It's important for everyone involved to define a set of pre-approved, objective criteria for judging what's presented, to avoid Design (or Copy or Strategy) Battleship. It eliminates, or at least reduces, subjectivity. Evaluate design choices based on criteria such as alignment with the overall strategy of the project; feedback received from representatives of the target audiences; functional requirements; user experience principles, etc. As we like to say, "every pixel (and ink dot) should have a purpose."

How do you arrive at such an ideal state? As it is in so much of what we've included in this book, the answer lies in information and how to act upon it. And where does one get such information? Research, friends. Research.

Start With Strategy

As we've seen, a strategy doesn't have to be complicated. It's just about creating an approach to solving a problem. However, as we've also seen, a good strategy needs to be based on a thorough understanding of the problem you're trying to solve. A clearly defined strategy can serve as a benchmark to evaluate every decision related to your project.

There are five dimensions for creating a strategy:

1. **Problem:** What's the problem you're trying to solve? Why does it need to be resolved?
2. **Product:** What is the product you're designing? Whether it's a website, an ad, or a brochure, it's important first to agree on what to produce.
3. **Audience:** Who is going to purchase or consume the product? It's vital to define whom you're creating for—and why.
4. **Market:** What's the context for the product? What are the external forces at work? Who are your competitors?
5. **Internal situation:** What forces are at work within the institution? What processes and procedures are impacted? What institutional roadblocks might stand in the way?

When you acquire actual information—as opposed to opinions—for each dimension, you'll reap some benefits: Generate new ideas, giving you the core insights and productive brainstorming sessions. Invalidate old, outdated ideas that people cling to out of habit and fear, rather than tangible results. Best of all, it will give you the understanding you need to develop iron-clad strategies to guide your process.

To get the information you need, you have to do research. But before you jump in and start writing surveys, you need to know what you're trying to understand.

A CLEARLY DEFINED STRATEGY CAN SERVE AS A BENCHMARK TO EVALUATE EVERY DECISION RELATED TO YOUR PROJECT.

Follow these four steps to developing a good research plan:

1. **Understand the problem;**
2. **Understand the desired outcome(s);**
3. **Understand what you're trying to measure (and why); and**
4. **Understand how you're going to collect data.**

It is a deductive approach, moving from the big picture (understanding the problem) to the specific (measurement and methods). We find this is a useful technique for projects with a limited scope; gathering information to test a hypothesis or solving a problem.

An inductive approach, going from specific observations to general observations/theories/hypotheses, may require additional time, effort, and money. (For instance, conducting a field ethnography to form theories about the behavior of specific groups.) It doesn't mean it's useless…just beware.

When crafting a research agenda, it's often useful to summarize the four questions in a simple document to ensure that everyone is, literally, on the same page. Here's an example:

What problem are we trying to solve?	Why is enrollment declining in our graduate programs?
What kind of outcome(s) do we hope to achieve with this research project?	A better understanding of the external forces/trends that might have an impact on graduate admissions for our institution (and our peers).
What does our research need to measure for us to better understand this problem?	Recent enrollment trends (within 2 years) in similar programs.
How are we going to collect the data we need and why are those methods going to be best?	A review of third-party research seems to be the most cost-effective way to tackle the issue. We'll pay particular attention to reliable third-party sources, most likely government information providers.

Getting the Data You Need

Once you've decided what you're trying to learn with your research, then you have to figure out how you're going to get it. Doing so requires a research method.

There is a broad range of research methods to choose from. You can do one-on-one interviews; conduct focus groups; send out surveys; or review third-party research to gain context. The right tool for you will vary. Some research methods are excellent at obtaining generalizable, "big picture" data about subjects that are tough to quantify (e.g., focus groups and impressions about design). Others are good at delivering narrowly focused data from large groups (surveys). The method(s) you choose depends on what you need to develop your strategy, available resources, and accessible populations.

Sampling

Unless you have a huge budget or an incredible research topic (e.g., "The Attitudes and Opinions of Institution X's Geography Faculty about the Recent Departure of the Department Chair"), chances are that you can only reach out to a subset of your audience. That's OK. It's still possible to draw useful conclusions from a representative sample.

But how many people constitute a sample? If you ask a statistician, prepare yourself for a lecture on "statistical significance." Ask someone who conducts usability testing and they'll tell you that fewer than ten (usually 7) suffice.

In practice, the ideal sample size depends on a combination of resources and needs. A discussion about calculating statistical significance is outside the scope of this book, but we're willing to risk the ire of statisticians everywhere by saying the practical answer is usually "enough to feel right." Generally speaking, you can get a feel for what seems to work based on your experience and industry-standard best practices. When in doubt, a quick trip to Google to seek out studies that are similar to yours should inform your target sample size.

Use one of these common methods to choose your sample:

- **Convenience:** i.e., "who can we get in the time we have for the money we want to spend?" If you don't always have a database of research subjects, recruiting subjects often depends on human factors such as availability, proximity, and attention. And you're usually stuck with whomever you can get.
- **Random sample:** If you have access to a pool of potential subjects, use some randomization method to get a useful sample.
- **Systematic:** Begin with a random selection at a starting point in your potential research subject pool. Then use a systematic

method to choose the other subjects. (E.g., every fifth person on a list after the randomly selected subject.)

- **Stratified sampling:** Used most frequently when you have to be sure that all members of a particular group (e.g., a political affiliation) are represented in the final research sample.
- **Cluster sampling:** Similar to stratified sampling, this is useful when you have to develop a sample that includes a subset of the population with a particular characteristic (e.g., prospective undergraduates living in rural counties in a given state with ten rural counties), choosing a subset of this group (5 of the ten possible counties), and then testing everyone who matches the criteria in the selected subgroup.

There are many issues surrounding sampling. They can (and do) fill the pages of many textbooks. However, you should at least be aware of the issues that make developing a representative sample—or, at least, what feels like a representative sample—difficult:

- **Missing elements:** You can't find the people you're looking for in your database or you can't locate them using recruiting techniques. You could go back and try to cast a wider net, but if you can't find the subjects that work for you, you may want to reconsider your research project.
- **Foreign elements:** You end up with members of your sample who don't belong there for a number of reasons, including incorrect data collection; deliberate misrepresentation by research subjects; or unclear recruiting instructions.

IN PRACTICE, THE IDEAL SAMPLE SIZE DEPENDS ON A COMBINATION OF RESOURCES AND NEEDS.

- **Duplicate elements:** It's not uncommon for people to show up more than once in a database. Make sure to scrub your database of duplicates before you start.

Research Methods

Once you've decided who you're going to look at in your research, you have to determine the method to use to get the data you need.

Which one's right for you? It depends on who (or what) you have access to, your resources, and what you're looking for.

Here are some of the most common research methods used by marketing and communications folks:

- **Qualitative:** If you're looking to get an idea of the "big picture" or get input on difficult-to-quantify subjects (design, brand experience, etc.), you'll probably be served best using qualitative research. While other elements in this list are classified as "qualitative," what we mean is sitting down and talking to people. This can take several forms:
- **Surveys:** After qualitative research, surveys are probably the second most useful research method when gathering data about the behavior, attitudes, opinions, and experience of a sample of a particular population. Typically, surveys are administered in a systematic way, often providing the subjects with multiple-choice questions.

  Surveys have the advantage of being easily administered to a large number of subjects when they're conducted remotely such as over the telephone, online via email or social media, or on paper through the postal mail. However, limitations are dictated by the breadth and quality of the questions included in the survey.

  Creating good surveys is both an art and science that is far outside the scope of this book. If you're interested in using surveys in your research (and you don't possess an advanced degree in statistics and market research), we urge you to seek out the services of a competent, experienced market research professional. They may cost more upfront, but when it comes to yielding beneficial results, it's a worthwhile investment to pay someone who knows what they're doing.

  CAUTION: While we don't have the space to dig deep into issues around survey design, please remember to avoid open-ended, "fill in the blank" questions at all costs. It may be tempting to try to gather more nuanced qualitative data, but we can assure you that it's not going to work. These types of questions are incredibly challenging and time-consuming to analyze. And, if you administer your survey in a "self-service," remote format (e.g., online), a good number of participants won't answer them. Do yourself a favor and don't include many (or, ideally, any) open-ended questions in your surveys.

- **One-on-One Interviews:**
  Researchers sit down (either in person or remotely, using the telephone or another form of
  one-on-one communication such as Skype) with a list of questions or a discussion guide that serves as a touchstone for the conversation. One-on-one interviews are useful for situations where you have:
  1. A small sample size
  2. Important individuals who can either offer significant information on their own and need to recuse themselves from influencing a larger group discussion (e.g., people in leadership roles).
- **Facilitated Discussion Groups:**
  If you have a large number of people to hear from, or if you want to gather multiple perspectives on a particular topic, a group discussion is incredibly useful. However, you have to be careful to assemble a representative sample of the group you're researching and be aware that people often behave differently in groups rather than participating in a one-on-one session. We always find it helpful to assure discussion group members that their answers will remain anonymous, and that we'll avoid using direct quotes in our final report. Remember: college campuses are small places!
- **Focus Groups:**
  A focus group moderator tends to guide the conversation around a particular set of questions. We find the rigid, systematic focus group methodology to be a lot less useful than a well-moderated, flexible discussion group.
- **Observation/Ethnography:** Observing research subjects in their natural environments is a type of qualitative research, but we're listing it separately because the primary objective of the observational study is to gather data about subjects in their "natural surroundings" without direct intervention. This method can yield some very valuable data, but it's important to recognize a few issues:

1. Your presence always skews the results. Unless you take great pains to hide (we like to dress up as trash cans…nobody pays attention to trash cans!), subjects who are aware they're under observation may behave differently in your presence.
2. Observational research is a more inductive approach that can, by its nature, take a long time to yield the information you want—if it yields anything at all.
3. To be truly effective, observers should receive training on both observation and data recording before going "in the field."

- **Historical:** Sometimes it's useful to eschew live subjects for the historical record. This type of research can be very useful when it comes to providing context, and it has the added benefit of not having to deal with the idiosyncrasies of live human beings.
- **Case Studies:** Researching case studies created by others (or studying your prior case studies) is a good way of providing broad context that ranges across multiple institutions, situations, or initiatives.

Those are the basics. While we probably haven't provided enough here to make you into a market researcher, we hope that you have sufficient information to appreciate why research is so important in the development of your marketing strategies.

TOOLING SURVEYS

Obviously, research can help develop the kind of understanding you need to develop a marketing/communications plan that works. But it can also be a marketing tool.

A respected business school came to us with a simple question: why are we having a hard time recruiting students for our executive education program? Executive education programs are pricey, and they're often paid for by companies interested in professional development. To find out why more companies weren't taking advantage of our client's tremendous offerings, we had to get to those who held the purse strings: human resources directors.

We crafted two surveys: one went to potential executive ed. The other went to HR directors at their companies. The survey, sent via LinkedIn InMail, was relatively brief and asked: What can you tell us about your reimbursement policies for professional development? We also tacked on one final question: Can we contact you about programs that you're offering?

The results exceeded everyone's expectations: more than 40% response rates from both groups. It turns out that large companies were most likely to pay for professional development. And they wanted some very specific training, mostly centered around technology and leadership.

By the end we had two things: great insights into what our local audiences wanted and a whole bunch of leads representing HR directors who wanted to know more about the program.

THE INPUTS: UNDERSTANDING YOUR INITIAL CONDITIONS

Building a solid structure requires understanding the environment where it will be built. Just as igloos don't tend to last long in the tropics, breezy cabanas are usually frowned upon as ideal living structures if you're building in a place where the temperature can drop below zero and the sun doesn't shine for months at a time. A structure that's going to perform the best is one that's built for the conditions you have.

Building a strong marketing plan using the OpenEDU model is no different. If you're going to create something that gets you the results you need, you first have to understand the institutional environmental factors you face. In the OpenEDU model, we call these environmental factors "inputs" and focus on the four most important ones:

1. **Budget:** how much money do you have to work with?
2. **Time:** how much time do you have to work with? And at what time of year will you deploy your plan?
3. **Goals:** What do you want to accomplish?
4. **Brand:** How do you want your audiences to feel when they encounter your organization? "Brand" is a big enough topic that we'll address it in the next chapter.

Budget Basics

Goals should be independent of time and budget, right? After all, a goal should encompass what we need to achieve, not what's possible. Wrong.

Budgets are destiny. They represent choices that will inevitably impact outcomes. After all, why spend the time (and money) engineering a regional branding campaign that includes expensive Out Of Home (OOH), radio, and television tactics if your budget really only supports a couple of print ads in the local newspaper's educational supplement?

But it's wrong to think of "budgets" as "lists of expenses." What you do to market your institution in order to increase awareness and drive enrollments is an investment in the future of your institution. Sure, marketing plans require money up front, but if you do your job correctly, return on investment will be many multiples of what you spent.

We think this bears repeating: marketing expenses are investments, not costs. Pitching your budget as an investment rather than a cost can help leadership loosen their death grip on the purse strings. This approach may also buy you patience and time—requirements for all great investments to mature and pay significant returns.

You'll need to plan for two primary investments: professional services and media. Professional services include research, strategy, creative, production, media buying, reporting, and ongoing support. Your media investments will cover the advertisement placements if your plan includes paid media. But not all plans include paid media. For example, you might focus efforts on earned media such as organic social media, search engine optimization, email marketing, public relations, and grassroots outreach. Remember, though: just because you're not paying for media doesn't mean it's free: even unpaid media efforts require people's time. When budgeting, consider your human resources too.

Media is often the biggest investment in a plan. Savvy partners will negotiate great media rates and added value on your behalf. And while it might have been the norm in the past for the folks planning and buying your media to be compensated by taking a commission on the value of that media, this isn't the case anymore. Insist that your partners don't charge a commission: a fee-for-services approach is a lot more honest (and transparent).

COUNTING PENNIES

After presenting the outcome of the OpenEDU model at the American Marketing Association's annual Symposium for the Marketing of Higher Education, an elite University in the Northeast asked if we could help market some of their programs. We said, "sure."

The school was intrigued by our success with email marketing strategies to generate "request for information" submissions. We reviewed their enrollment goals and timeline. We also looked at the programs in question, the challenges the programs faced and their marketing strategy, destination and nurture strategy.

We recommended focusing most of the limited budget and time on an email campaign. We knew that by using specific email lists we can typically cut out a year of the lead to enrollment cycle by reaching a targeted audience that is further along in the decision-making process.

We drafted a series of emails for each of the programs and used URLs with tracking as well as offer codes waiving the application fee to help drive leads.

We designed our landing pages to collect leads for the primary programs we were marketing first. Upon submission of the inquiry form, a confirmation page suggested other, similar programs worth considering in this graduate school. The campaign yielded direct enrollments thanks to the application fee waiver code and related programs.

We saw a 23% lead to started/completed application rate within the first six months of the overall campaign. In fact, some programs saw 31% of all form submissions resulting in applications.

Budgets range across institutions. In the corporate world, marketing budgets should be about 5% of the company's gross revenue to retain the current market position. Businesses that are looking to grow or gain market share budget 10% or more of the gross revenue.

For-profit universities might play at the corporate level, but most colleges and universities can't afford it. While well-funded schools typically have $3MM to $5MM in their annual marketing budgets, many schools can make magic with budgets ranging from $500K to $1MM.

When your budget is limited, your best bet is to go digital, focus and stagger your buys. Digital media is more economical, by and large, than traditional media. It allows you to hyper-target sophisticated segments, and it can drive more action than traditional media in the short-term.

Focus your marketing on promoting specific programs that perform well traditionally and have "infinite" operational capacity or highlight programs that are struggling—but don't spread your small investment too thin by marketing everything all at once. We guarantee that this won't be a politically popular position to take, but it's the only one that makes sense. If you get pushback from the smaller programs that feel that they're being left out, you may want to gently point out that office and classroom facilities on campus are not allocated equally to each program either.

When you don't have a lot of dough to amass a significant showing, take a staggered approach. Set your media flights for every other day, every other week, or create a solid block of three to four weeks that leads up to a major milestone in your enrollment timeline.

Pro tip: Squirrel away 10-to-15% of your budget. Sometimes projects run hot, and you'll need the extra scratch to keep the campaign running. However, make sure that you're familiar with your institution's policies about money that's "left over" at the end of the fiscal year. If you're in a "use it or lose it" situation, it doesn't make sense to leave money on the table. If you can't figure out how to spend it, you may want to consult your finance folks for creative (and above-board) ways to keep the money in your budget for later use.

Getting Time on Your Side

Time is another major investment. You have to plan for three timelines: research/planning, creative, and the media flight.

Depending on how much primary research is necessary, the research and planning phase can take anywhere from one to four months. Once research and planning is complete, you can start creative.

Creative development may be fast or slow since it's often an extremely subjective process. The number of creative deliverables and approval processes that often include multiple administrative (and sometimes academic) units can also make the creative phase sluggish. We've found that the stronger the research, the easier it is to move through creative because research reduces subjectivity: while a 55-year-old professor might not like a certain creative approach, if you can show that your focus groups of actual prospective undergraduates reacted well to it, it's a lot easier to overcome objections.

A high degree of collaboration between the creative and business teams (internal, external, or both) also helps move creative development forward. Make sure the creative team writes a strong creative brief that's substantiated by the research. Schedule collaborative sessions where creative and business viewpoints can be aired. Be honest with your feedback. Keep the lines of communication open at all times. Test concepts with target audiences if you have

TIME MATTERS

When a small public university in the Midwest contacted us, they wanted a quick campaign. Previous attempts at reaching out to prospective undergrads had fallen short and they were worried they weren't going to reach their goals. Worst of all, they were running out of time. The recruitment season was well underway.

Obviously, the need was urgent. But we didn't realize how urgent until they told us we had weeks to get a campaign up and running. We made it happen because they were willing to collaborate closely with us in order to make the best use of the time we had. We both knew we were running out of time and the work took priority for everyone involved.

We had to prioritize. We worked together to identify the programs that would yield the best results; the audiences that were most likely to respond; and the message that would resonate with those audiences in order to drive them to take action as quickly as possible.

We identified the elements of their brand experience that would spur action. We collaborated to brainstorm creative approaches that would get us the results we wanted.

The client arranged a photo shoot featuring actual students, and we developed the creative assets we needed in one day. With a strong brand platform for our work, we were able to quickly transform those elements into action-oriented ads that could be deployed across both digital and print platforms. And then we flighted.

The results exceeded expectations. Even though we worked fast, we never lost sight of the core elements: brand and audience.

the budget. Make sure that every creative decision is backed up with real-world data. If everyone acts on good faith, relies on the research, and communicates with each other, the outcome will invariably be something you can all be proud of.

It might take two to four weeks to conceive, create and produce a straightforward display banner campaign for a single program—provided there is good research, available photography assets, and a minimal approval process. The creative for a comprehensive integrated advertising campaign that includes radio, billboard, display advertising, search engine marketing, social media marketing, email, and some OOH (bus shelter and bus-backs) could take anywhere from two to four months. Make sure you build in production time when creating your project timelines.

Doing good work takes time. At this point, from start to finish, you could spend as much as six months before you are able to launch your campaign. But, as we pointed out earlier, time is just as much of an investment as money: it's always better to spend more time to do it right—as long as that time is spent wisely.

Pro tip: Get into a routine. Schedule a standing daily, weekly or biweekly meeting with all parties involved to align, prioritize and commiserate. It doesn't matter when you decide to have your call, what matters is that you make it a habit. Even if all you have to talk about is the weather, the discipline is healthy for the project and it will keep everyone on track.

Goals Matter

Time and time again, when it comes to goal setting, reality has a way of pulverizing idealism. To paraphrase W.B. Yeats, no matter how good our intentions might be at the beginning of the project, things have a tendency to fall apart in one way or another under the pressures and requirements of the real world (see our "Structured Flexibility" case study on page 69 for some strategies to deal with chaos).

The OpenEDU Model is engineered to be realistic. That's why "goals" follow "budget" and "time." Usually the budget is what it is. Time marches on no matter how much we may wish otherwise. And the academic year is going to happen on the same schedule, whether we're ready or not.

Goal setting can be a tricky business, especially when you throw in the constraints of time and budget and the constantly moving target of institutional priorities. Your best bet is to keep your goals simple and explicit. For example, "increase awareness" is simple but not explicit: Increase awareness among which audience? Why? Over what period of time? Measured by what metric? By how much?

Be clear and precise about what you're trying to accomplish. It will be easier to decide what to keep and what to drop during the planning phase.

Be mindful of your audience. Chances are that at some point you will feel pressure to run expensive and potentially wasteful media just to appease people who are probably not the target audience (ahem...faculty, administration, trustees, etc.).

Unless these groups somehow magically align with your recruitment, retention, or awareness goals, it's worth the time and political capital you'll need to expend in order to fight a good fight and save your precious media money to spend on the right people—your intended audience. Senior administrators will forgive not seeing a billboard advertising your school on their way to work sooner than they'll forgive declining enrollments (or, worse yet, bad publicity) because of a botched recruitment marketing campaign.

Goals can be accomplished *synchronously* (i.e. at the same time) or *asynchronously* (not always together). For example, it's not unusual to want to

POINT & FOLLOW

You've probably never heard of thanatology. But that's o.k. Most people haven't. And that was our challenge.

A large public institution with a well-respected professional graduate program approached us with a well-defined goal: recruit 12 students into our new thanatology graduate certificate program.

First, thanatology wasn't exactly an easy sell. Defined as "the scientific study of death and the practices associated with it, including the study of the needs of the terminally ill and their families," it's a discipline that few would consider mainstream.

We knew that there had to be a market. We just had to find it. But our clients' focus on a specific goal, coupled with their knowledge of the market, made filling this new program a lot easier than it would have been if everything hadn't been clearly defined. In the end, we created a brand platform rooted in caring and compassion during death and dying. Then we targeted audiences involved in professions that focused on those life stages and built a media plan that worked to efficiently accomplish the goal by focusing on paid search emphasizing keywords such as "nursing home jobs," "hospice," etc. Within the first six weeks, we delivered 80 leads from our search campaigns at a cost of just over $41.00 per lead.

Our client contacted every lead by phone the moment they came in. As a result, we got regular feedback related to the high quality of the leads generated. When the program was over, we'd done it: we'd recruited the 12 students they needed. It wasn't easy, but without a clearly defined goal it would have been a lot harder.

promote specific programs while building awareness for the institution as a whole.

This kind of approach clears the way for the subsequent program-specific marketing with serialized goals such as:

- Over a six-month period, increase local (define local) awareness by 15% among undergraduate prospects, as measured by an awareness study. Then, once awareness is on the way up…
- Work to increase qualified leads for a specific undergraduate program by 50% over the next few months, as measured by leads year-over-year during the corresponding period.

These are sequenced goals. Parallel goals have similar properties, but they run concurrently.

There are a lot of ways to set marketing goals, but no matter how you approach setting your goals, make sure they're realistic, well articulated, adequately funded and properly timed. If your goal is longer than one sentence and it doesn't roll off the tip of your tongue, rethink it. You'll be glad you did when you're able to keep everyone involved in the project focused on that shared vision.

Case Study: Structured Flexibility

Have you ever taken the time to craft the most elaborate, logical, and realistic project plan? Was it chock-full of tasks and subtasks, milestones, dependencies, effort time, resource assignment, resource allocation and utilization? If you were extra careful, maybe you even factored in the team's planned vacations, national and religious holidays, and anything else that could impact your carefully planned sequence of events.

You might have even done project modeling and articulated the critical paths, calculated slack and modeled what it would look like if you had to "crash" the project. We're sure your plan was a perfect, true, bulletproof work of art. But it wasn't. Something—or lots of somethings—happened along the way making your carefully crafted plan seem like a sick joke.

In our experience, the most beautifully designed project plans are the first to fall apart. Perfectly planned projects have a tendency to collapse under the weight of expectations and wishful thinking. Life's never perfect anywhere else. Why should you think that your project's going to be any different?

When it comes to planning a project, our first commandment to our team and clients is "Thou shalt leave thine ego at the door." This commandment isn't intended to prevent anyone from feeling proud of their work or deploying their expertise. We want that. What we don't want is close-minded thinking or planning based on the ol' "it's always been done this way" model.

To combat over-planning, over-promising, and unfulfilled expectations, we've developed a project management process called, "Structured Flexibility." And it works.

"Structured Flexibility" is more of an attitude than a process. It's not a concrete series of steps that can be learned or boxes that can be checked. In fact, it's designed specifically to combat the kind of task-focused linear thinking that inevitably leads to trouble and tunnel vision.

It's a way of approaching project based on the work of the two professions that probably understand the futility (and arrogance) of assuming we can foresee everything in advance: the military and improvisational theater.

At West Point, soldiers learn a concept called "Commander's Intent." In this concept, high-ranking officers articulate high-level objectives (the *what*) to soldiers on the ground who are responsible for accomplishing these goals (the *how*). For example, if ordered to "take that hill," the junior officers on the ground with their troops can consider conditions that may have changed since the original assault plan was created. This creates an initiative to choose a new route that allows them to flank the enemy in order to complete the objective. The key idea here is that the plan isn't the goal…the goal is the goal.

Improvisational actors, by definition, improvise based on conditions such as audience input, scene changes, or other environmental factors. However, "improvisation" doesn't mean "anarchy." Instead, people doing improv adhere to one simple rule: "Yes, and…".

Responding to unexpected changes with a "Yes, and…" mindset forces actors to accept what's going on and then develop solutions on the fly that allow them to advance the discourse positively and intelligently.

A mountain of work has been done on the psychology and physiology of positivity—and at the risk of sounding way flakier than we actually are—we've seen amazing, productive, collaborative results with our clients and partners by using this technique.

When someone says "Yes, and…" they will collaborate on a solution, it's the opposite of responding to changes with, "No, that's not what we agreed on." "Yes, and…" prompts solutions. "No" draws lines in the sand that someone must cross if the project is going to move forward. And "No" inevitably leads to hurt feelings and damaged relationships.

The Fourth Input: Brand

Brand *is*.

Yup. It's really as simple as that. Your institution's brand exists whether or not anyone's taken any active steps to "create" it. If your institution exists, you've got a brand.

It may sound strange to anyone who's still clinging to the notion that "brand," as derived from the marks that cowboys seared into their cattle, somehow has to be wrapped up in a well-defined visual representation. And even if you don't recognize yourself in that statement, if you still use words like "brand" to stand in for your logo—or if you talk about "branding" as a design exercise—you're still clinging to the idea that "brand" and "logo" are, if not synonymous, closely related. You probably also think that your institution's brand is something you can control, either by adhering strictly to a set of guidelines or keeping a close watch on how various academic and administrative units use (some say "butcher," but we think that's kind of harsh) your institution's logo, color palette, or, in some cases, tagline.

Certainly, "brand" as a controllable (if indefinable) thing that can be created, expressed in various media, and unleashed to the world under tightly controlled conditions is a very good idea that can be pretty comforting to those of us who self-identify as "marketers." Unfortunately, it's wrong…and it's always been wrong. To learn why, let's take a brief detour and look at where the whole concept of "brand" came from in the first place.

Linguistics and Listerine

The concept of "brand" has been with us throughout human history. As soon as people gave each other names (or even just named the group they belonged to), they created a link between one thing (a name, a sound, a symbol) and a set of tangible and intangible attributes that differentiated one thing from another.

Meaning is a little more complicated than the simple equivalency between a word and an ideal image shared by people trying to communicate with each other. Context can make a difference too. "Meaning" is contextual, and because it's contextual, it's inseparable from culture.

Joseph Lawrence was an American living in the 19th Century who was smitten by two recent scientific breakthroughs: Louis Pasteur's ideas about infection and Joseph Lister's discovery that carbolic acid could be used to kill germs. Lawrence developed a mixture that seemed to do as good a job killing germs as carbolic acid. He licensed the formula to a pharmacist, Jordan Wheat Lambert, in 1881. In honor of Lister's work, the Lambert Pharmacal Company began marketing the mixture as Listerine. They promoted it as a wonder formula for everything from cleaning your floors to cleaning your, ahem, nether regions to making your breath sparkling fresh.

Unfortunately for Lambert, Americans didn't think they had a problem with bad breath. It just wasn't a thing . . . until Jordan Lambert's son, Gerard, came along.

Gerard Lambert realized that if Americans didn't think they had bad breath, he needed to convince them that they did. While digging into medical literature he chanced upon the term "halitosis," a previously obscure word used mainly by doctors who needed to describe particularly rank bad breath. Gerard then launched a barrage of advertising designed to "educate" the public about a problem they didn't even know they had: "chronic halitosis."

Gerard Lambert's campaign relentlessly called out the social problems associated with bad breath. Mothers were told that their children secretly couldn't stand to be around them because their breath stank. Young men and women were told that nobody wanted to marry them because their mouths smelled like sewers. Women with bad breath were painted as social outcasts whose friends talked about them behind their backs. Who would want to be near someone whose breath made them sick?

The impact of the campaign was immediate and spectacular. In seven years sales of Listerine shot up from $118,000 to more than $8 million. "Halitosis"—a condition nobody knew they had prior to the campaign—became a household word. Listerine was on its way.

Looking back now, the Listerine campaign looks pretty unsophisticated and, to be honest, fairly offensive. By taking a word that was basically unknown to the general public (and therefore neutral when it came to any emotional associations) and linking it to shame, social ostracism, bad health, and general failure, Lambert was able to construct a reality in which "halitosis" became Public Enemy #1, and Listerine was the only product to cure it. Modern advertising was born!

"Reality" 101

But does just saying something make it so? While it may be tempting to believe that anything repeated loud and long enough will become reality to the people receiving the message, the truth is that creating meaning is a lot more complicated and, as we've seen, tightly bound to a wide range of cultural, aesthetic, and practical factors. It may not be enough just to create the right message. It may also depend on who believes it or not.

While we'd all love to have a simple formula that guaranteed the reality we're constructing around our brands always took hold and spread to our target audiences, the truth is that constructing reality is messy. People don't always behave in predictable patterns. Some ideas take hold and others don't. And the reasons usually have to do with an infinite number of cultural variables that are completely out of our control. We can build it and they will come . . . or not. So what to do?

Understanding Your Brand

In the OpenEDU model, "brand" is the fourth input that influences what you ultimately create. And while concepts like "budget," "time," and "goals" may be easy to understand (and communicate to others), "brand" is lot harder to get across. Not only are most definitions of it pretty slippery, but the word has been so misused in popular culture that people often equate

TRICKY THING

A brand is a tricky thing. Every institution has one (whether they like it or not), but it can often be hard to define in a way that's true to the values of the institution and appeals to those who don't know the school. This is especially true if a school's core values might lead to preconceived notions.

We faced this challenge when working with a small, private, Catholic college in the upper Midwest. The institution had existed for more than a hundred years, and we knew that people who were unfamiliar with the brand might be turned off by the school's religious affiliation and perceived values. It was our job to figure out how to remain true to the college's brand and mission while creating a brand experience that appealed to a wider range of prospective students.

To do so, we had to get to the core of who they are. We interviewed leadership, administrators, faculty, and students in order to better understand what the campus experience. We examined the content on their site and what they sent out to prospective students. We researched what kinds of values might appeal to prospects. And then we sat down to think.

Rather than couching the brand with language that screamed "Catholic," we were able to distill the brand down to three words that spoke to the values of the institution in a way that resonated with their heritage and appealed to the interests of today's prospective students. Those few short words spoke to a wide range of hopefuls.

"brand" with "logo," a construction that couldn't be farther from the truth.

When it comes to understanding the Fourth Input as it applies to your marketing efforts, it's important to realize that a brand is what happens when your institution comes into contact with the myriad audiences who connect with it. As we've demonstrated in this chapter, that experience can never be the same for any two people. But you can still define its main characteristics and use that definition to inform how you construct your marketing plans with the OpenEDU model.

Consider how your institution's brand distinguishes itself. How does your school differ from your competitors? When people visit for the first time, what kinds of impressions do they come away with that they wouldn't find on a competitive campus? If you can answer these questions, you'll be a lot closer to understanding your institution's brand. The other way to approach the brand definition is to approach it from a more prosaic angle. Why do people choose your institution over your competition? Or, alternately, why do they go somewhere else?

When you examine this question it may be tempting to stop with answers such as "cost" or "location" or "the majors we offer." But these are just signifiers. To understand them, you have to look at these reasons from the standpoint of your prospective students. What does "cost" mean? There are certainly always cheaper alternatives—especially in the age of MOOCs—for anyone who wants to be better educated. When it comes to your school, what does "cost" really mean? Does it really mean "value?" Does it mean "investment?" Are prospects who choose another institution really saying that what they have to pay for your institution isn't worth it because of the kinds of jobs graduates get, the network of alumni they'd have access to, the quality of instruction, or how readily they'll be able to apply what they learn to the "real world"? The answer will get you one step closer to understanding how your prospects perceive your brand.

THE THREE PILLARS

In the OpenEDU model, your plan is constructed from three pillars and capped off by a strategy that guides your efforts. In this section we'll explore the three pillars of the OpenEDU model and how they come together to create a marketing plan that works for your institution.

The Three Pillars in Action

Our model includes three tactical pillars: traffic, destination, and nurture. *Traffic* is driven to a *destination*, for example, a recruitment landing page. It is then essential to *nurture* your arriving audience to achieve your desired outcome.

We're sure you've got the idea of the three pillars by now. Here's how they work in practice.

Traffic

Traffic is the area where you will make the biggest investment. Some traffic-generating tactics are very expensive (e.g., TV advertising); some aren't (e.g., paid search). There are loads of options and you may be tempted to hedge your bets by spreading your money around equally to as many as you can afford. Don't.

The key to generating traffic effectively is timing the deployment of multiple tactics to maximize impact through an integrated marketing push. Done right you can create synergies between media, ending up with an impact greater than the sum of each of the parts.

For example, if you're running an outdoor media campaign, consider also (if you can swing it financially) releasing mobile banner and text ads with the same creative/message and call to action. The traditional media push will lower the digital campaign's click barrier by increasing familiarity with your brand among target audiences, and digital outreach will similarly enhance the effectiveness of traditional media, adding value to each rollout.

Flexibility is another key to effective traffic-generating campaigns. No plan is bulletproof. Some program aspects may penetrate more quickly or effectively than others. Designing your strategy to incorporate flexibility will be crucial to your ability to respond in real time to the ongoing results of your efforts.

Traditional media still offers the greatest opportunity to broadly disseminate your message. Unfortunately, most traditional media outlets, such as TV, radio, out of home (OOH), and transit don't allow for a lot of flexibility (if any) to change creative content during a campaign's run. If your traffic-generating plan includes traditional media (and most likely it will), make sure you think through each media outlet's restrictions, including limitations to cancellations or mid-run changes to the media flight. In cases where the medium presents such barriers to creative flexibility, focus that portion of your integrated marketing on brand awareness and basic messaging. These are less likely to change once the campaign is in full swing.

Digital media, on the other hand, can combine the flexibility you need with a more targeted version of the mass-communication qualities of traditional media. Digital radio, digital billboards, and video pre-rolls, to name a few, allow for hyper-specific audience segmentation, and also let you increase, decrease, suspend or shift your spending based on performance. You can't always use digital media, but when you do, your campaign benefits additionally from its capacity to support both branding and directly actionable audience engagement. In other words, digital allows you to augment the branding power and reach of traditional media with greater flexibility, targeting, and real-time performance optimization.

OUR MODEL INCLUDES THREE TACTICAL PILLARS: TRAFFIC, DESTINATION, AND NURTURE.

Always keep timing and flexibility in mind when engineering traffic-generating media campaigns. If and when possible, design campaigns for double duty: build awareness via traditional mass marketing—and swap digital creative in and out at a moment's notice.

Destination

Destination could mean an open house at your student center, a conference room in a hotel (i.e., a traveling open house), a page promoting a particular degree program, a landing page focused on a particular action (e.g., make an appointment with an admissions counselor), or even the homepage of your website. Regardless of the particular destination, each must be designed in a way that supports your brand, message, and goals, and each must be engineered to spur further action.

The term "destination" implies specificity. Just as you can't buy a bus ticket to "west," your traffic can't or won't arrive without a clear understanding of where it wants to go. The goal of every destination is to educate, refine traffic flow, and lead further. Based on our experience, simply sending traffic to your homepage and hoping for the best is the least efficient way to generate a desired outcome.

While there is a great deal you can do to optimize your digital destinations, take care to align Admissions team talking points with up-to-date branding and marketing efforts. Train anyone who will interact with your audiences until your messaging is second nature, and craft prompts that will help your representatives move prospects down the "sales" funnel.

If your destination involves live interaction in a physical place, come prepared with enough people (e.g., admissions representatives) and stuff (brochures, viewbooks, applications, etc.) to engage the people that you've driven to the location (i.e., your traffic). If you can, offer "live online" or traveling events that replace the need for prospects to come to campus. We've helped clients set up on-the-spot admissions interviews, "instant admit" events and information sessions.

And, by all means, build data collection into all destinations. You can't know what's working and what's not—and adjust your marketing tactics accordingly—if you don't have the data to back up your decisions.

Nurture

If *destination's* job is to collect leads, then *nurture's* job is to convert those leads. After developing destinations that help achieve your goals, focus on creating an internal communications campaign that nurtures leads through the sales funnel of applying, accepting, and enrolling.

There is plenty of evidence that supports the obvious: the faster you follow up with prospects, the better your chances of converting them. It's critical that the nurture campaign's timing and content are crafted to move prospects along at the right times with the right actions. Don't just consider when and how often you can follow up with prospects. Know what you will say at each touch point.

Nurture flows can include direct mail, email, and telephone calls. Consider designing them around seasons, application deadlines, or other time-based events. Make sure your lead-nurturing plan aligns with your branding platform and answers the questions your audiences care about. Most importantly, stage the flow so it feels as clear and comforting as possible.

We call this tactical pillar "nurture" rather than "push" because the continued flow of traffic to destinations must be regulated with an exhibition of care. Think about a road trip: the longer you go without clear signs, the more likely you are to assume you're lost. Each nurture email or ask must be associated with clear calls-to-action that do not push audiences beyond their current comfort level.

Deep Dive: Traffic In The Digital Age

The most visible (and measurable) part of any marketing campaign is the traffic that it generates. Being able to do something out in the world and then seeing that effort bear fruit in the form of people coming to your website, leads pouring in to your admissions office, or people showing up at an open house is pretty heady stuff. It's the kind of thing that sets marketers' hearts aflutter. It's measurable. It's real. It's something you can report to your boss.

However, the concept of "traffic" can be a lot more elusive in the Digital Age. "Attention" and "engagement" can be difficult to measure, and raw numbers alone aren't always a reliable indicator of whether your traffic-generating efforts are working. Taking an action online requires very little effort.

In this section, we'll dig into some of the difficulties you might face when trying to generate traffic. Then we'll offer some suggestions for dealing with the somewhat ephemeral nature of "traffic" in the digital world through the lenses of mass media, direct response measured in "clicks," search marketing, social media, and content marketing.

Attention in the Multi-Screen Universe

For many, the hardest part of dealing with the realities of today's multi-screen media universe is getting over pervasive preconceptions about how media works.

UNFORTUNATELY IN TODAY'S MEDIA UNIVERSE, THINKING IN TERMS OF DIVISIONS IS DEAD WRONG.

When it comes to advertising, most of us have been brought up to think of "media" as being comprised of several totally separate realms. At the highest level, there's "traditional" vs. "digital" media. Dig down into "traditional" and it's typically divided into television, print, outdoor, and radio, which are considered mass media platforms. "Digital" is a little more complicated, but we can start with "mobile" vs. "web" and then break up each into smaller pieces based on format: "display," "search," "in-app," etc.

Considering how we divide things—and, to be fair, we're often forced to, based on how media is bought and sold—it would be easy to think that each medium and format within that medium exists on its own. Television is separate from the radio. Search is separate from online display advertising (a.k.a. banner ads). Mobile web advertising is different than mobile video advertising, etc., etc., etc. No surprise. You probably experience it every day.

Unfortunately in today's media universe, thinking in terms of divisions is dead wrong.

But don't feel bad: it wasn't always this way. At some point in the past, this kind of thinking was unavoidable. But the world's moved on. We're in a whole new media universe.

The Rise—and Fall—of Convergence

Two things occurred that ushered us into the new media age. The first step was the digitization of nearly everything that came about as a consequence of the mass adoption of the Internet and the World Wide Web. Tim Berners-Lee invented the web because he was looking for an easier way to share scientific papers with his colleagues at CERN. As usage increased, people began to realize that they could use the web to publish original content, and publishers discovered another channel for what they printed.

Innovative people quickly realized that the web could serve as a publishing platform for *anything* digital. Video, music, games, animation, and other digital content started to appear. While technology and bandwidth may have initially limited the spread of digital content, early visionaries saw the potential and ran with it. In fact, Pseudo.com, the world's first online television network, was founded in 1993 and attracted millions of users before going down in spectacular flames during the dot-com bust of 2000. (Check out the excellent documentary *We Live in Public*—http://documentarystorm.com/we-live-in-public—to learn more about Pseudo.)

Over time we began to understand the web as a *meta-medium*, delivering everything that all "traditional" media offered in one place. There was even a word for it: *convergence*. The TV and the computer merged, letting us live happily with one big screen in the living room that gave us all the content we could consume.

But a funny thing happened. New types of screens started to pop up, allowing us to access content over the Internet in a way that didn't feel like using a computer or watching a television. These screens were a lot smaller, more portable, and, well, more *personal*.

First smartphones let us access Internet content anytime and anyplace we had a cellular signal. Then came tablets—not the wonky "personal digital assistants" of the late 90's (remember the Palm Pilot?) or the clunky "tablet PCs" of the early 2000's—but thin devices with relatively large screens and long battery life (compared to laptops) that allowed us to curl up with "e-books" in a way that approximated a print book, surf the web from the couch or the bed without overheating laptop batteries burning our legs, and play games just by touching the screen. They turned on instantly, ran for hours, and were literally so easy to use that a baby could use one. Heck, there are even iPad games designed for *cats*.

Instead of one screen "convergence" we have something very different: multiple screens that allow us to multitask our content consumption in a very personal way. It disconnects content from the limitations of time and space.

"Web" content, once consumed only at a desk in front of a computer, is viewed equally well on a bus, on a couch, or from the beach. Advances in streaming media make television and radio content accessible from anywhere on nearly any device, effectively freeing the media from their eponymous containers. New "time-shifting" technologies (e.g., DVRs) allow us to "tune in" to content whenever we want, and providers like Netflix and Hulu free us from the tyranny of network programming schedules and video rental services. We have media on demand, anytime, and virtually anywhere.

The portability of these new devices also introduces a new dimension: simultaneous screen usage. Sure, in the past you could sit down at the computer and watch television . . . as long as they were in the same room. Laptops helped pave the way, but they're still gigantic and clunky compared to a smartphone that fits in your pocket. The advent of the smartphone and tablet marked the beginning of our current multi-screen universe. And its reality may be a lot stranger than you think.

Through the Rabbit Hole

The first symptom that times were changing is the fact that younger people—usually the earliest adopters of new technology—have been slowly cutting down on their television consumption over the past several years. According to aggregated viewer data from Nielsen, in the first quarter of 2011, 18-24-year-olds watched an average of 26 hours and 28 minutes of television per week. By Q1 of 2015, that number had dropped to 18 hours and 4 minutes. All other age groups show similar—if less precipitous—declines in TV viewership.

Where's that TV time going? According to recent research published by Millward Brown, it's pretty clear that our attention is being directed to mobile devices. In fact, according to their study, consumers spend more time on their smartphones each day (151 minutes) than their televisions (147 minutes). Laptops (103 minutes) aren't all that far behind, but at 43 minutes per day, tablets still have a way to go to get their share of our attention. In any event, our usage of screens other than TVs has increased 157% since 2010.

But the really profound change is that we're spending our time using all these screens simultaneously. The amount of our time is still up for debate—the Millward Brown study found that 41% of screen use takes place simultaneously, but a study by Microsoft found that an amazing 70% of consumers used a second device "in some capacity" when watching TV. Either way, our attention is becoming increasingly fragmented.

Television seems to be faring the worst. In a laboratory study conducted by YuMe, a multi-screen video advertising technology company, it turned out that while test subjects favored TV the most, compared to other devices (53% of the time), they also spent less than half the time paying attention to it when other devices were available. In fact, the YuMe study found that the attention span while watching television dropped from the initial rate of 53% to a dismal 19% after only 4 minutes of simultaneous viewing.

Why does our attention wander away so quickly? The Millward Brown study may provide some answers. When survey participants were asked why they were using other devices while sitting in front of the TV, 43% responded that they wanted to "fill time"; others (38%) were keeping up with their friends on social media; 30% didn't like being saddled with having to watch something that someone else in the room had chosen; 26% said they were "busy and just needed to get things done"; and 21% admitted to "being bored with TV."

There is one additional reason that says more about the state of audience measurement and advertising effectiveness than any other: 36% percent of Millward Brown study respondents admitted that they weren't ever really watching TV at all. It was "just background noise."

CHANCES ARE GOOD THAT THE TV IS ON BUT, ATTENTION-WISE, NOBODY'S HOME.

Why is this a big deal? Simply put, if these numbers are generalized to the entire TV watching population (or, at the very least, the 64% who own smartphones), it means that a big chunk of the TV audience doesn't "consume" it. Chances are good that the TV is on but, attention-wise, nobody's home.

So what's a marketer to do in the multi-screen world of today? Sadly, the answer for many seems to be to just throw up as much ad content as possible across as many screens as possible in hopes that it will "stick," a sentiment echoed by consulting giant PwC in their most recent Global Entertainment and Media Outlook report:

"Internet advertising will increasingly become device agnostic... advertisers should be asking what types of content generate greatest consumer engagement rather than whether people are reading a website on a mobile device or not."

On the surface, this prediction seems to make sense. After all, isn't the idea of deploying content across multiple devices the whole idea behind the explosion of "responsive design"? But when you dig deeper, the cracks really start to appear.

First, let's consider why people use smartphones in the first place. When the Pew Internet and American Life Project looked into the topic, the answers weren't all that surprising. Regardless of age, text messaging, Internet use, email, video, and music were some of the main reasons along with, of course, voice and video calls. To "avoid being bored" was again the top choice as to why people picked up their phones, though younger people (18-29) were much more likely to admit to using the phone to entertain themselves (93%) than people over 50 (55%). Younger people also used their phones to escape their current circumstances more than older folks: 47% of 18-29-year-olds admitted checking it to "avoid others," compared to 15% of the 50+ group.

Microsoft's study dug a little deeper, determining that simultaneous screen use could be classified into four categories:

- "Content Grazing" (68% of respondents): Engaging in behavior to distract themselves.
- "Investigative Spider-Webbing" (57% of respondents): Gathering information on a topic or discovering new things (e.g., researching actors on IMDB.com while watching a movie).
- "Social Spider-Webbing" (39% of respondents): Connecting and sharing with others while doing something else.
- "Quantum" usage (46% of respondents): "Sequential, content-based" browsing, moving from one link to another.

The "social" aspect of simultaneous screen usage bears special mention because it seems to be a catalyst. However, "social" depends on what's being watched and when the consumer is reacting to it. A study by ShareThis (reported on ClickZ.com) found that screen usage seems to match the characteristics of the channel. Twitter, with its rapid-fire format of 140- character messages, spiked during live events. Reddit, a social network that looks a lot more like old school discussion boards and lends itself to longer posts requiring more time (and thought), peaked immediately after an event.

The Four Dimensions of the Multi-screen Universe

If all this sounds scary, frankly, that's because it is. It's virgin territory, terra incognita, unknown and unmapped, and we're all pioneers in the multi-screen universe.

Dimension 1: Audience

We have to know whom we're trying to communicate with. It's pretty clear from the research on screen usage that factors, such as age, socioeconomic status, gender, and ethnicity influence which screens people use and when. For some—particularly younger, non-white people with low incomes and low levels of educational attainment—their portal to the digital world is most likely smartphones, according to Pew. More affluent people might be more likely to have more screens available. However, usage seems to correspond mostly to age, which also affects our second dimension.

Dimension 2: Intention

The reason someone is using a particular device has a big impact on where they are in the multi-screen universe. If they're engaged in researching products and/or services; creating content other than photographs or video; or working, chances are that they're using a desktop or laptop computer. These devices, with multiple inputs (mouse, keyboard), large screens, and high storage volumes lend themselves to such activities. On the other hand, if they're commenting on a movie they're watching, entertaining themselves while waiting in line, trying to navigate their physical space, or documenting their travels, most likely they're using a smartphone or tablet.

Dimension 3: Context

Context, where someone is (or their circumstances) also influences what people do and which screen they choose. Teenagers stuck watching the news with Grandma will be on their phone as soon as they can sneak it out. If they're at work (and actually working), they'll be on a desktop or laptop machine.

Dimension 4: Device

The characteristics of a particular device will influence the user behavior. Smartphones, with their portability, always-on data connection, and a trove of preferences and data, become very personal. (Microsoft's report uses the Jungian archetype of "The Lover" to characterize the role smartphones play in our lives.) It translates to frequent usage over the course of a day as a connector, boredom-killer, on-the-spot advisor, and navigator. On the other hand, laptop and desktop computers function as tools of creation, portals to information, number crunchers, and organizers of all the information we collect throughout our lives. (Microsoft assigns them to the Jungian archetype of "The Sage.") Tablets are somewhere in between, performing many of the functions reserved for laptops and desktops in a personal way.

Targeting in the Multi-Screen Universe

Once we identify the values of the four dimensions to locate a target, we can use those coordinates to develop communications that work best.

For example, you want to reach 16-to-18-years-old who are searching for colleges. Since you know whom and why, you can infer context (probably at home) and device (laptop or desktop computer). Why? Because they need to research large amounts of information and organize it for future reference. You can assume that they're at home because research shows us that if they're out and about, they're probably using their smartphones to access the Internet for something other than looking for a college.

- **Audience:** Prospective students between the ages of 16 and 18 who are interested in attending college.
- **Intention:** They want to pick a college that's right for them.
- **Context:** In their homes (or primary domiciles) focused on searching.
- **Device:** Laptop or desktop, either in a bedroom or a communal area in the home.

So what do we do with this information? First, use what you know about your audience to craft a message. Next, since they're engaged in a search, consider a paid search or listings on college ranking websites. At home, they probably have time to read more information than if they were on their phone. And they may be able to share their findings with an older adult. Finally, a laptop or a desktop machine translates into more processor-intensive, immersive experiences, such as high-definition video or graphically intense interactive experiences (e.g., virtual tours of a campus).

On the other hand, let's say that the same prospective students have chosen a set of schools to visit and they're on their way to campus for the first time. You can safely assume that they're in the process of traveling and using a smartphone (or possibly a tablet with a cellular data connection) and adjust your dimensions accordingly:

- **Audience:** Prospective students between the ages of 16-to-18 who have developed a "short list" of schools to visit.
- **Intention:** They want to pick a college that's right for them.
- **Context:** Traveling to campus for a visit.
- **Device:** Probably a smartphone, though possibly a tablet with a cellular data connection.

In this case, the audience needs information in small chunks to help them get where they're going, find who they're supposed to meet with, navigate around campus and the surrounding area, and maybe share what they're doing with their friends and family.

An app or a well-made responsive site optimized to provide navigational and contextual information on a small screen is the most effective means of communication for this situation. You have their attention already, now you need to convert them from "prospective student" to "applicant."

Ad Astra Per Aspera

In Latin, "*ad astra per aspera*" translates roughly as "to the stars through difficulties" or "a rough road leads to the stars." In either case, it's an inspirational phrase that tells us we have to put up with a lot of tough stuff before we reach the heavens.

We're just beginning to navigate the unknown lands of the multi-screen universe, and it's not easy. Considering that the first generation iPhone appeared in 2007 and the first-generation iPad launched in 2010, we're at the very early stages of understanding the impact these nearly ubiquitous devices will have on communication, entertainment, and, even, culture. What happens to face-to-face relationships when we can connect digitally with friends 24/7? How do separate viewing screens and replacing the television (the family's "hearth" for decades) affect family cohesion? Will the ability to transmit a continuous stream of real-time information about what we're doing change how we navigate and relate to the world (see Periscope)? And what will happen to the first generation that grows up with the world moderated through all of these screens?

It's impossible to tell, but we can start mapping this unknown territory.

Ditching the Click

Imagine that you're the V.P. of Communications at a Washington, D.C.-based organization tasked with influencing national policy on a specific issue. Then, one day, after months of hard work developing your online audience, you've finally done it: Your Twitter feed has a follower.

You might be asking, "Why would anyone be so happy about one stinkin' follower?"

Advertising metrics grew out of one stark reality: we didn't know who saw our ads. Sure, we could use some sophisticated statistical techniques to make educated guesses, but specifics were a technological impossibility. It was an open secret that audience measurement in the pre-Internet days was more shared fiction than reality.

Marketers used a shotgun approach, blasting out numerous ads to enough people in hopes that we hit at least some of our target market. It was all about "reach" and "frequency": how many people got hit and how often we blasted them.

That approach was the norm for decades, so it made perfect sense that when the web came along we just kept doing the same thing: get that ad out there in front of as many people as possible, as many times as possible. But that was just the start. The web was going to revolutionize the ad industry because not only could we put ads out there—we could tell how many times they were clicked!

But what did clicks really measure? The assumption was that a click was the equivalent of someone showing interest. And that was important.

Unfortunately, most of us realized that getting clicks wasn't enough, especially if they just dumped people on the home page. What we wanted was a click to turn into a lead or a sale. We wanted something to happen. Oh, and we also wanted the ads to impact the brand by raising awareness or changing brand perception.

Strangely, the metrics didn't change. Some publishers and ad networks started offering cost per action or cost per acquisition (CPA) models, but they were expensive and difficult to measure. Google changed the equation by offering the cost per click (CPC) model and others soon followed. While it was a revolution at the time, we continued to focus on clicks. It was quantity, not quality—metrics for an action that may not mean anything at all.

That may change soon.

The *Financial Times* and *The Economist* recently announced they will move towards a Cost Per Hour (CPH, Yay! Another acronym!). The metric focuses on the amount of time an ad is in front of readers.

It remains to be seen if other publishers will get on board, but if advertisers like it you can be sure others will follow. After all, it's actually a bit of a throwback to the way TV advertising is priced, a point not lost on Shenan Reed, president of the media-buying firm MEC North America. Quoted in the *Ad Age* article announcing the move, she predicts, "[CPH pricing will] be more like TV with metrics [advertisers] can understand and can relate to."

IF YOU CAN'T RELATE TO ONLINE METRICS TODAY, YOU'RE PROBABLY IN THE WRONG BUSINESS.

We argue that if you can't relate to online metrics today, you're probably in the wrong business. But the idea of going back to a time-based model surely must give a lot of folks the *warm 'n' fuzzies*. After all, it's what many of us—especially those of us who remember the days before the web—first experienced.

Besides being a nostalgic, feel-good method, CPH pricing may also have a number of other positive consequences, including encouraging engagement with long-form content, that could drive the development of higher-quality content to hold viewers' attention longer—a development worth getting behind. As *Ad Age* points out, it may encourage creatives "to take digital display ads more seriously" (another positive development). Driving longer engagement via CPH pricing may also increase brand recall: the *Financial Times* found that readers who experienced an ad for at least 5 seconds showed a 79% increase in recall.

The real key, however, is that it could be a major boon for publishers. The web is awash in page views (we're looking at you, Huffington Post slideshows) and many publishers find themselves suffering from excess in unsold or deeply discounted inventory. And why shouldn't they? After all, "pageviews" are a virtually unlimited resource.

Time isn't, however. Tony Haile, the former CEO of Chartbeat, a major digital analytics company, notes that "time is the only unit of scarcity on the web."

"You've only got 24 hours a day per person," he says, "That directly correlates with the goals of advertising. Just like any economy of scarcity, anyone who captures the most of it can charge more."

He's right, of course. TV and radio ads are priced on a model that recognizes that time is money. And as more and more sites and apps fight for our attention, time is a resource that's getting scarcer every day.

We still don't think that it's measuring the right thing.

Is going back to the future with time-based advertising the panacea for all online advertising woes? We don't think so. Maybe the Holy Grail of online advertising isn't about measuring *what* people do, but *who* they are.

Remember our example at the beginning of this section? If you were trying to influence a national policy and your one Twitter follower was the President of the United States, you'd be pretty happy. It's definitely one case where the quality of your audience matters a lot more than its quantity.

Current metrics value the President's clicks or time-on-page the same as anyone else's. But if the President sees your message, the potential to make an impact is astronomically greater. Our country may have been founded on the premise that "all men are created equal," but when it comes to marketing, some clicks and views may have a larger influence.

THE STUFF THAT WORKS BEST ONLINE IS THE STUFF THAT CAN ONLY WORK ONLINE.

Clicks or time still require a shotgun approach when it comes to advertising. Sure, targeting and behavioral targeting algorithms are getting more sophisticated. But most publishers and ad networks still base their pricing on the assumption that we can't tell exactly who we're marketing to. That's not always true.

There's one adage about the digital world that we believe to be true: the stuff that works best online is the stuff that can only work online. Online success doesn't come from "porting" content or business models from one medium to another but, rather, creating new content and business models to take advantage of the unique properties of digital media.

While advertising models that look at actions are a step in the right direction, they need to include a dimension that considers the quality of the person taking the action to offer more than "traditional" direct marketing techniques. Pricing ads based on the time they're on a visitor's screen might be innovative and could potentially change things for the better, but it seems like even more of a throwback to another medium. On the other hand, combining these measures with an additional dimension that takes into account the quality of the person interacting with or seeing the ad is something that truly takes advantage of "digital" characteristics in a way that's not possible in any other medium.

"How is this different than targeting?" you may ask. Good question.

It's different because it combines techniques to determine differential pricing based on multiple factors. By pulling these factors together—action, time and identity—it would be possible to price ads on how much they're worth to the client, rather than what percentage of screen time, screen space, or mouse clicks they consume.

We may not be there now, but as more sophisticated tracking techniques such as canvas fingerprinting and Big Data-based behavior profiling (not to mention the wealth of personal info in social media) become more available, the potential exists to finally achieve the dream of advertisers everywhere: reaching the right person with the right message for the right amount of time to drive them to take the action you want them to take.

Earned and Paid Search

There are two kinds of people in this world: those who want to find their own answers and those who want to be told the answer. The people who want to find their own answers almost can't trust the answer unless they found it themselves. In the context of web search, these fine folk prefer to sift through organic search results. They are not in the minority either. According to a recent Forrester Research study, 54% of people prefer to find information naturally using search while 18% prefer sponsored ads.

The interesting thing about the people who prefer natural search results is that while they do want to work to answer their own questions, they don't want to work too hard at it. 71% of people will never make it past the first page of search results. They will either pick one of the first ten options or change their search. And since 51% of all website traffic comes from organic search, it's important to optimize your Search Engine Optimization strategy.

Search result ads fill a need for the people who want to be told the answer. They figure, often correctly so, that these ads are here because someone thinks their information will meet the needs of the end-user. And if it doesn't, they'll just bail at no cost to them.

In the end, however, these two types of people are not orthogonal about how they answer their questions. Some organic searchers click on ads; some ad clickers also click on organic search results.

Marketers should consider running both paid and organic search campaigns concurrently if there is enough in the budget to support both activities. When funds are short, read up on basic SEO tactics and implement the fundamentals on your own. Once you get past the basics of SEO, there is a ton of advanced trickery that can be implemented to gain additional traffic. Considering the time and money to manage, track, and adjust advanced SEO on an ongoing basis, you are likely to get more bang for the buck with paid search.

Paid search can be very expensive, however, and wasteful if it's not done correctly. There are many factors to consider and tune on an ongoing basis that could make anyone's head explode. If your budget allows, the best bet is to hire a certified, honest search consultant to do the work on your behalf.

Sometimes, even with the most expert help and great lemons, you still can't make lemonade. If there is a low search volume for a particular search term or phrase in your demographic and geographic target, there is very little that you can do to substantially increase qualified traffic to your destination. You can always broaden the targeting by using looser terms or relaxing the demography/geography. When you do that, however, you'll generally get less quality traffic that will invariably impact your quality scores and drive up your media cost.

Unfortunately, optimizing for organic search position is also expensive. Whether it is done in-house or you employ a consultant for the search, it takes time. A lot of it. The cost of internal resources is sometimes easier to swallow than paying for an external resource. And as long as the internal resource has the training and support to do this activity well, this can be a fine way to get it done.

Here are some key concepts for SEO:

- Benchmarking is key. Know how you stack up against your competition by using tools such SeoMoz or Spify
- Scrub keywords
- Check your sitemap XML
- Look for broken links and errors—and fix them
- Use H1, H2, page titles, file names, etc. correctly
- Consider Local Listing, YouTube, Google+

Findability is a team sport. If you can swing it, use both paid and organic search to help prospects find you.

Social Media

It's a pretty sure bet we all agree that social media has become a key component of any organization's marketing plan. In 2017, marketers are expected to spend $13.52 billion on social media marketing initiatives in the US, a number that's projected to rocket up to $17.34 billion in a couple more years. And while surveys may vary slightly when it comes to who's using social media marketing, it's probably pretty safe to say that 92-to-100% of marketers are turning to social media as a new way to reach their customers and prospects.

But is it working? In the 2014 Social Media Marketing Industry Report, only 34% of the 2,800 marketers surveyed felt that their

Facebook marketing was effective. The well-respected CMO Survey, conducted by the faculty of Duke University's Fuqua School of Business, found that social media performance was pretty bleak, with only 15% of the Chief Marketing Officers surveyed reporting that they could prove the ROI of their social media marketing efforts. Given these numbers, it's probably no surprise that a recent Forbes survey found that 70% of CEOs think their company is wasting money on marketing initiatives. Social media may contribute a lot to CEO marketing angst.

Of course, there are plenty of anecdotal examples of social media campaigns that have been hugely successful. Brands are getting results. But for every social media superstar out there, we'd bet you a donut (available weekly at idfive, by the way!) that there are literally thousands of brands out there struggling to make social media work for them.

If we want to understand why social media isn't working for many, perhaps it's best to start by asking what it is that marketers are trying to do with social media. And while asking ten marketers this question will probably yield you twenty answers, the 2014 Social Media Marketing Industry Report found that the number one question was pretty simple: how do we, as marketers, use social media to engage with customers?

Seems like common sense, right? After all, isn't it the promise of social media that it's going to help us engage with our customers and prospects in a way that's never been possible? Isn't it right to ask that they just "Like" or "Follow" us and maybe engage in a little bit of conversation now and again? We all know that if we can get them to interact with us, they're ours, right?

Maybe not. To answer that question, it's important to first look at how consumers form opinions about companies in general. If we can understand that, we surely can figure out how to use social media.

So what really matters to consumers? A recent study published by the Society for New Communications Research found that the top five influencers of consumer attitudes were:

- Quality of products and services: 80%
- Cost: 55%

- Customer care programs: 37%
- What family, friends and trusted people say about the company: 34%
- Customer reviews and ratings on social media sites: 30%

Seems to make sense, right? We've all been there: we want quality, service and the opinions of other people who matter to us. It's common sense.

Even in the offline environment, the same qualities seem to make a big difference. In a recent survey of consumers that looked at why they shop retail (rather than online), a big chunk of them said that what they were going to the store for was to get something that's often difficult to get online: access to help and advice from knowledgeable sales people. Unfortunately, almost three- quarters of them ended up frustrated because the salespeople didn't seem to know anything about the products, didn't know what else was in the store, and hadn't the foggiest notion what was in stock.

Unfortunately, even with all the lip service being paid to "customer engagement" and the power of "conversations" we're having with customers and prospects online via social media, the online experience doesn't usually seem to be much better. A study by Social Media Marketing University, earlier in 2014, found that companies basically suck when it comes to responding to complaints or even comments from customers…the very stuff that social media is supposed to be all about.

Examining the question about how brands responded to customer feedback in social media, the survey found that while 60% of participating companies reported receiving customer complaints via Twitter, less than 20% responded immediately to this kind of customer input.

With this kind of disconnect, it's no surprise that 25% of the companies surveyed in the study reported that they had lost revenue due to unfavorable "buzz" on social media.The survey then asked consumers how they felt about these interactions and the results weren't pretty. Seventy-two percent of consumers indicated that they expected quick responses to complaints voiced in social media, with an astonishing 60% reporting that they'd be likely to take "unpleasant action" if not responded to right away.

The problem with social media begins to look even bleaker if you study the E-Expectations Report from Noel-Levitz. While this survey of more than 1,000 students (and their families) concentrated on the college search process that high school students were going through, its findings seem to make a lot of sense in just about every industry. And it provides some helpful glimpses into exactly what so many marketers are getting wrong when it comes to social media.

The first indication of what's wrong is their finding that social media from colleges is the least influential of all online media when it comes to forming opinions. While 75% of the survey respondents reported that the websites of the colleges they were looking at influenced their decision to attend, less than 20% indicated that Facebook had a positive impact.

Clearly, they're looking at social media. But why doesn't the social media marketing being thrown at them have any impact?

On the surface, it gets even stranger when you look at how the people who responded to this survey "engaged" with social media. Approximately 37% of the survey respondents reported "following" colleges that interested them on Twitter (up from 25% in 2013) and 51% reported that they visited a college's Facebook page. Clearly, they're looking at social media. But why doesn't the social media marketing being thrown at them have any impact?

According to the survey, their decreased willingness to engage is one of the significant reasons. While 55% of survey respondents reported "liking" a college in 2013, the number plummeted to 35% in 2014. Another 35% reported doing "nothing." When asked why they didn't engage, most responded that they were afraid of clicking "like" because they didn't want to share personal information with the colleges they were looking at . . . a pretty reasonable approach considering what goes out in social media today.

And herein lies the entire problem with social media marketing (and why many of us are doing it wrong): we want to engage with them, but they don't want to engage with us.

Sorry. They're just not that into you.

The notion behind social media marketing is that brands can easily engage with their customers. The reality (for the most part) is that they don't want to. Sure, they expect us to engage with them when they complain or ask us for something specific, but they're not all that interested in an ongoing dialogue.

However, a recent study on Millennials and social media sharing by ShareThis found that social media sharing could have a huge influence on purchasing behavior when it comes from a peer. In fact, 70% of those surveyed reported that they made a purchase based on content shared by a peer via social media!

But it also turns out that what and where they're sharing makes a difference. Entertainment content was much more likely to be shared on Facebook, while content related to business, finance and sports was more likely to be shared on Twitter. Meanwhile, Pinterest owned shopping with a 238% higher "sharing" rate than Twitter or Facebook.

If you think about it, it starts to make a lot of sense. Entertainment content that doesn't require a huge amount of time and can generate a lot of social conversations (music videos, film trailers, cat videos, etc.) ends up being shared on Facebook. More timely content about "the facts" turns up on Twitter. And our consumer habits and aspirations are broadcast to the world via Pinterest.

But whichever way they're sharing, one thing is clear: they want to talk to each other, not to you—the brand. Things are shared because they serve a social purpose, not because they want to form a deeper relationship with the organizations, brands, and companies that consumers come into contact with. The hard truth is this: they don't want to be your "friend."

This kind of behavior makes even more sense if you look at a recent paper published by the Pew Internet and American Life project that used network visualization to identify various patterns in Twitter networks. While the researchers identified six distinct conversational patterns, two, in particular, seemed to address specifically how consumers interact with organizations and brands:

- **Brand Clusters:** This type is formed around products and celebrities. These popular topics attract large fragmented Twitter populations, generating mass interest, but little connectivity.
- **Broadcast Network:** News media outlets and pundits that have loyal followers who retweet them trigger this type of event. These communities are often star shaped, as little interaction exists among members of the audience.

In both cases, very little "conversation" or "engagement" took place between the participants and the object of their admiration. In the "Brand Cluster" networks, consumers discussed brands with each other in small communities. In the "Broadcast Network" structure the interactions were distinctly one-way, with one major hub in the center sending information out to followers (who interacted very little with one another). Neither structure is what any of us would call a "conversation."

So is social media marketing a lost cause? Not at all! As we've seen, social media can have a huge influence on the brands and products that people like and buy. But in order to make it work for you as a marketer, you have to accept one hard truth: consumers don't want to talk to you until they want to talk to you. Trying to force the issue with ham-handed attempts at "engagement" isn't going to work. However, you better be ready to talk to them when they want to talk to you.

It's not hard to do social media right. In fact, trying too hard to be "social" while neglecting the "media" might be the biggest problem. Here are seven things to think about when constructing your next social media campaign:

- **It all begins and ends with content.** "Sharing" happens among networks of peers because people want to share. Give them something worth sharing. Skimping on production, creativity, and audience focus when it comes to generating content for your social media presence means that you're just wasting your time (and money).
- **Make it easy to share.** If you have a website, do everything you can to make your content easy for people to share. But don't force it down their throat. Include sharing links everywhere you can. Make compelling images (or infographics) that are "pinnable." Create short, tweet-friendly URLS. Whatever you can do to grease the wheels of sharing is something that's going to help get your content out there.
- **Understand that you're a small part of their world.** It might be your life, but they're not going to think about your company very often. Unless you're a major affinity brand like Apple and Disney or a sports franchise, don't expect them to think about you until they need you. Bombarding them with irrelevant or forced content isn't going to get them to love you more.

- **Respond quickly.** Your customers will talk to you when they want to talk to you. If you're not there to respond, you're going to create some serious ill will.
- **Provide value.** Make 'em laugh. Give them something to think about. Make them say "hmm." Whatever, but it should be valuable to them and their social networks.
- **Respect privacy.** People are getting pretty savvy. You can't trick them into receiving your stuff. If they don't feel that their privacy is being protected (selling, ahem, your list, ahem, to third parties), then they're probably inclined to go away.
- **Success = sharing.** When it comes down to it, if people are sharing your stuff in their own networks, you're winning. "Likes" and "follows" don't really count.

It isn't tough, but it appears that many of us have been doing social media all wrong. It is about conversations—just not with us (until they want to reach out to us).

Content, not Containers

One thing that the digital marketing industry is superior at is taking old ideas and renaming them so that they seem hip and new. Think that "social media" is new? Folks who lived in the San Francisco Bay Area were posting messages back and forth to each other on the Community Memory system in 1973. Still trying to wrap your head around email marketing? The first use of electronic communication to send messages for advertising a service occurred in 1864. A dentist in England thought it would be a good idea to send a mass telegram to politicians advertising his services. Are your designers still trying to figure out how to create effective banner ads? AT&T placed them back in 1994, more than 20 years ago!

So when we encounter the hype around "content marketing," many of us who've been around the online block more than a few times tend to roll our eyes jadedly. After all, the Ancient Roman government used newsletter-like bulletins posted around cities as a way of communicating with their subjects. Heck, even if you want to strictly limit your definition of "branded content" to "content being used to market a company's products and services through mass-produced printed materials," all you have to do is check out the magazine *The Furrow,* produced by John Deere, the tractor manufacturer, to see an example of "content marketing" that's more than 100 years old.

But just because the ideas aren't new doesn't mean that they're useless. What we call "social media" may not be entirely new, but today's social media connects close to 2 billion people around the world, making it an incredibly powerful channel for reaching your prospects and customers. While the entire "email marketing" (OK, telegraph) industry may have consisted of only one pioneering dentist back in 1864, today 73% of marketers report that email marketing is "core to their business." And banner ads have arguably come a long, long way since the first one asked us the radical question, "have you ever clicked your mouse right here?"

Content marketing is no different.

Today, 79% of marketers report that they're using (or moving toward) content marketing as a regular part of their marketing mix.

While B2B marketers are often seen as lagging behind their B2C colleagues, a survey from the Content Marketing Institute found that 91% of B2B marketers are using branded content. Across all sectors, 78% of CMOs surveyed expressed the belief that "custom content" represents "the future of marketing."

Why so much interest? Simple: it works! Leads generated by organic search—one of the prime benefits of content marketing—have been shown to generate a close rate nearly 15 times higher than other outbound sourced leads. Content marketing taps into the consumer purchasing decision early, long before they're even thinking about talking to a sales person, boosting the likelihood that brands using content marketing are more likely to "make the list" than brands that aren't. And in a world where consumers are increasingly distrustful of news media as sources of information, a recent study of consumer trust found that corporate content is one of *the* most trusted sources of information.

But just because content marketing can be an effective tool in your marketing mix doesn't mean that you can just slap up some "content" and ride off into the sunset, secure in the knowledge that you've become a bona fide "content marketer." Like all marketing tactics, content marketing won't do anything for your brand if it's not implemented strategically. The web is littered with "viral" videos that weren't, and there probably isn't a single person reading this who hasn't encountered more than a fair share of ghost blogs, dead Twitter feeds, and zombie Facebook pages. While it's impossible to guarantee that your content marketing process will be effective, it's a sure bet that a content marketing process without a strategy behind it will leave you at a loss.

Case Study: From Digital Traffic to Foot Traffic

Getting thousands of people to the somewhat-rural campus of our mid-sized public university client wasn't going to be easy. Far from major transportation hubs, the school suffered from a lack of awareness. To add to the challenge, our client wanted to reach out into regional metropolitan areas, particularly to groups of prospective students.

Since we had to reach out to high-school students, we went where more and more of them spend their time these days: online streaming media. We chose one of the most popular free, ad-supported streaming music services because we'd been impressed with both their demographic reach and targeting abilities. We had used this partner in the past to deliver open house attendees and it was always successful. This effort was no exception.

The results were astounding. By the end of the multi-week campaign, we'd received thousands of RSVPs and had been able to direct interested students and their parents to transportation options for the one-day, campus-wide open house. When the big day came the campus was filled with more than 2,100 attendees, eager and ready to learn more about what our client had to offer.

The Second Pillar: Destination

Once you generate traffic, that traffic has to go somewhere. In the OpenEDU model, we call that somewhere "destination," and it's an integral part of any marketing campaign. After all, if you're not sending those whom you've enticed with your message somewhere they can take an action, you've lost them.

However, in order to understand how "destination" fits into the model, it's also important to understand that we're using a pretty expansive definition of "destination." While there are the obvious "destinations" a campaign could send traffic–landing pages, open houses, campus visits, calls to the admissions office–legitimate "destinations" can also include a prospect's internal conception of your institution (i.e., brand); what they say about your institution to others (i.e., word of mouth); or the pressure they exert on a prospect to add your institution to their considered set (i.e., influence).

Because defining "destination" can be elusive, outlining what makes a good destination can be pretty elusive too. In this section, we'll examine some of the factors that make up a good destination and offer suggestions for how to create destinations that get the result you're looking for.

Design Matters (More than Ever)

As the diversity of competition in higher education continues to rise and the cross-channel playing field of gaining raw impressions is further leveled, today's differentiator is no longer media budgets and volume of content; instead, it's the quality of your content and the fidelity of its presentation. Just as we witnessed in the early 20th Century through the Bauhaus and Modernism movement influences on hard goods such as housewares and architecture, today's coming-of-age of internet content emphasizes usability. This includes a push toward reduction in adornment, an emphasis on usefulness and function, and a natural pairing of form with function.

Bad design leading to a poor brand interaction in any touch point is not only a faux pas. It will no longer be tolerated or accepted as a symptom of engineering constraints.

"The design of everyday things is in great danger of becoming the design of superfluous, overloaded, unnecessary things."
– Donald A. Norman.

We've witnessed this shift already with many head-to-head, consumer-facing product battles. Of course, the original Apple iPhone launch stands out as the megaphone (pun intended) that told the world a highly technical and complex device didn't have to be confusing or ugly. Instead, it could feel natural to infants and the elderly.

Since then, Apple and Google have both defined the barrier to entry for digital brand experiences through their standardized, atomic user interface (UI) development kits. MySpace (remember them?) and their dancing GIF backgrounds were swiftly dethroned by a small startup project called Facebook that launched with a clean, minimal interface, hyper-focused on only a few utilitarian features that it did really well.

AN EXCELLENT DESIGN SERVES AS A FOUNDATION TO A RICH AND POSITIVE BRAND EXPERIENCE.

Today a new startup called LetGo is pointing and laughing at the rot Craigslist bestowed on itself through their indifference to interface and experience design beyond a desktop view. The minimalist Craigslist design reminds us that a good interface isn't "timeless" as audience and ecosystems evolve. In contrast, LetGo offers a beautifully simple and intuitive, geolocated app, to list and sell your stuff to people nearby.

New experiences come through new devices, and old interfaces appear weathered when they don't keep up with new contexts—the device itself, where, when and how it's used.

It's essential to realize that an excellent design serves as a foundation to a rich and positive brand experience. Higher education, in particular, already faces an uphill battle in getting the eyes of prospects and donors. If you squander the opportunity to build a lasting relationship with each of those leads when you finally grab their gaze, well, it's a complete waste of marketing dollars. Similarly, harkening back to Apple and Google, it's important to step back from any single brand touch point and see it within the context of a larger brand experience.

The brand is the way someone answers the phone or replies to an email. It's the ambient, on-campus experience including way-finding signage, informational handouts, and environmental graphics supporting our touted value statements. The brand is everything before and after a specific transaction.

Great design is thinking about that entire journey of many, intermingled brand experiences, to shape a larger, emotionally binding brand relationship that drives loyalty and leads to transactions. It's the filling of the proverbial "trust bucket" you'll dip into when you ask prospects and donors for something in return.

Fortunately, we don't have to upend our entire brand experience to make positive differences in engagement. Instead, we can select strategic touch points to attract new fans and, over time, shape our loyal base like a topiary as we gradually unify our brand.

360-Degree Experience Design

Today's web is a great metaphor for where marketing and brand experience has gone. Prior to the iPhone, the Internet was composed of web pages. As designers, we conceptualized websites and web pages in much the same way we conceptualized a 150-page annual report. The larger taxonomy of a site was considered from a lofty view, the content organized logically, and each page or template wireframed architecturally into the optimal layout. We built it, and it was done—at least until it became old and needed to be done again.

That reality was all too simple, even if the technology seemed difficult and fickle. All of that went out the window when we had to consider mobile as an alternative, adaptive platform. Then our foundation was further shaken when those polar platforms became a rainbow of devices of all screen sizes and capabilities—enter responsive design. Today, even the concept of a graphic interface is in question. Dubbed "the Internet of things," we now regularly interact with screenless fitness bands that track our body vitals and give us feedback, buttons on washing machines that order detergent by drone delivery, and a plethora of hardware devices that communicate with us in the home and on the go. As interface designers and innovators, we're now forced to think beyond the interface and reflect on what a brand experience is at its core—and how that translates to the online brand manifestations we will build next.

Even without knowing precisely where the Internet will go, or without having web "pages" already dissolved, ambient and intentionally invisible, communication has evolved with branding and advertising for more than a century. An emotional attachment to

Coca-Cola red is in the same vein as both Nike and Under Armour entering the fitness sensor market to fill out their brand ecosystems—or Disney personalizing their in-park experience with badges that identify patrons with costumed characters and exhibit displays.

In higher education, attracting prospects—donors, students, faculty, partners—will require thinking beyond websites and landing pages. We still use them as conversion touch points, but websites and landing pages are the bridges between other brand experiences, including digital and interactive experiences in lobbies and campus signage, updated call scripts, improved workflow design (for example, designing the follow-up schedules with leads), and even considering how everything can be personalized and naturally social. The higher education brand needs to become ever-present and accessible at the precise moment a prospect needs it, building deep, emotional bonds in the in-between.

The broadening and unifying of the higher education brand—the 360-degree design experience—will come via a handful of intentional efforts, including:

Think beyond the "graphic." Across print, broadcast, and digital, recognize your brand experience as everything in-between. Rethink tangible touch points and design collateral to support and extend larger brand and marketing efforts. Consider how a brand experience can be crafted through in-person exchanges, personalized environmental interactions such as on-campus displays, and non-disposable take-homes utilizing the capabilities of apps and devices.

Conduct field research. Run usability tests on today's applications to identify market and brand opportunities for improvement. Conduct prospect interviews, focus groups, and collaborative sketching studios with prospects and stakeholders, rather than following the higher education herd.

Understand, map, and redesign workflows. Use test findings to map out and understand internal and external workflows, journeys, and processes. Evaluate the day-to-day pressures and decisions of recruiters to build campaign and tracking tools that aid in relationship building. Understand the prospect decision-making journey and lifecycle inside and out in order to improve existing touch points and minimize possible prospects from falling through the cracks.

Establish and extend atomic brand libraries. Build cohesive brand UI libraries across digital applications and printed collateral—iconography, photography style, code components and widgets, grid systems and templates, and even content libraries to pick up brand language. A useful brand library is much more than fonts and colors. Build the library as a flexible brand foundation, not as a rigid, over-policed system, to make it easier for growth and refinement.

Identify and update key touch points. Review what you know about the workflows and journeys to pick low-hanging fruit or particularly problematic engagement points. Use them to develop new brand assets, new experiences, and better conversion tools one at a time. Avoid overhauling everything at once and encouraging failure.

"The ability to simplify means to eliminate the unnecessary so that the necessary may speak." – Hans Hofmann

Seasoned and experienced designers are the fuel for each of these efforts. Fill out your team with a blend of visual design skills, researchers and statisticians, interaction designers, and interface developers. A multi-disciplinary blend will be integral to innovating in the higher education space and to stop thinking about experience design as the next mailer or website refresh.

Tomorrow's successful higher education brand will step outside of specific deliverables to look at and understand their greater prospect wants and needs, to craft brand experiences and lasting relationships. Marketing budgets will be diverted to experience designers and researchers, to create fewer—but more potent—prospect conversion touch points that complement ambient efforts. Brand advocacy and social sharing will become your most valuable marketing properties, converted through on-point, well-crafted pages that pull and appear when the prospect needs them.

Case Study: A New Destination for A New Goal

Love 'em or hate 'em, *U.S. News & World Report's* rankings really do influence prospective student choice. And while most institutions struggle to move up the rankings, our client had a particularly difficult problem: how to stay at the top.

The answer might seem simple—just keep doing what you're doing—but the reality is a lot more complex. Rankings aren't just determined by objective criteria such as starting salaries of graduates or how long it takes them to get jobs. They're also determined by a number of subjective rankings, not the least of which is rankings from leaders of peer institutions.

We knew that we couldn't affect graduation rates or alumni success, but we did believe that we could have an impact on how the institution was perceived by its peers. And the answer wasn't redesigning the website. The current site was huge, and we'd never had time to change it in order to impact brand perception.

After much deliberation and collaboration with our client, the answer became clear: celebrate the accomplishments of the previous year. After all, the school was doing great work, conducting research and developing innovations that literally made millions of people's lives better.

But these discoveries and inventions weren't always front-page news. Many were the kinds of discoveries that only those in the field would understand and appreciate. They just had to know about them.

The end result was the creation of a website dedicated to chronicling the major achievements of the previous year, delivered in a way that reinforced the brand and positioned it as the leader in its field.

We went to work on two fronts. Our designers collaborated tirelessly to develop a way of presenting the stories in a fresh, contemporary way that also allowed us to tell a unified story. Our copywriters went to work mining the school's publications (both academic and otherwise) to uncover the biggest discoveries of the year. When we found them, we wrote them up in a way that would appeal both to the scientific community—a big part of their audience—as well as to an informed public of professionals in non-research roles who were also in the field. Then we combined the innovative design and content into a new website destination that told a cohesive story that encapsulated the school's previous year.

What we did must have worked, or, at the very least, contributed to their continued success. They're still holding the top position they've occupied for decades.

The Third Pillar: Nurture

OK. You've generated traffic. You've sent that traffic to a destination that engaged them enough to start a relationship with your institution, even if that "relationship" is nothing more (at this stage) than "send me more information." Congratulations! Now you're ready to nurture that relationship into something that bears fruit.

There are many, many ways to nurture a prospect into an applicant and, eventually, into someone who enrolls at your school. In fact, there are more ways to do this than we can cover in our book. But no matter how you decide to approach your prospects–email, live phone calls, text messages, engagements in social media, or a series of mailings–the first step to nurturing a relationship with them is to understand how they make decisions in the first place.

Understanding the Decision-Making Process

People are motivated by different things. Everyone processes information in their own way and they're influenced by various factors. Some decisions are made emotionally, as soon as the first foot touches the campus; others are an outcome of complex logic and reason. Nailing down a particular type of student's decision-making process is hard, to say the least.

Consider the diversity in just one factor, such as emotional intelligence, among a different topology of students: college prep, undergraduate, transfer, post-baccalaureate, graduate, post graduate, doctoral, post-doctoral, certificate, continuing education, and lifelong learner. That's just one dimension.

Now think about each of these types of students and consider how the psychographics change when you factor in a second dimension, such as the military. Then consider how an undergraduate candidate that is currently in the military makes an attend/not attend decision. And what would be the considerations of an active military service person to choose a post-baccalaureate, graduate, post graduate, doctoral, post-doctoral, certificate, continuing education, or lifelong learner program?

Let's keep going. What are the considerations for a young, middle-class, undergraduate, active military, African-American woman versus the concerns of a middle-aged, Hispanic, non-military man who wants to finish his undergraduate degree? Same school, same program, but these are widely different people with widely different reasons to go to school and finalize the decision-making process. And since they are looking for different things to finalize their decisions, marketers need to understand their audience segments—and cater to them.

The best way to convince people that you've got the right product for them is by actually having the best product for them—and then by telling them about it in a way that makes an emotional connection. To do that, brace yourself, you have to get to know your audience.

Figure out what they need and what they want (two very different things), and honestly assess if you can meet those needs and wants. If you can't do the assessment, don't spend any more time on them and move on to the groups that benefit from what you have to offer. Not every school is right for everyone. Once you accept that, you give yourself the permission and freedom to be surgical and effective.

> **THERE ARE MANY, MANY WAYS TO NURTURE A PROSPECT INTO AN APPLICANT AND, EVENTUALLY, INTO SOMEONE WHO ENROLLS AT YOUR SCHOOL.**

We might have lost some of our readers after that last paragraph, but don't give up on us until you read this next paragraph: Most—not all—schools are breaking their backs to meet enrollment goals. Enrollment goals roll up to total student population—a.k.a. total tuition revenue. As it turns out, there are three functions that can support total tuition revenue: Marketing (lead generation), Admissions (nurture leads through enrollment) and Student Services (retention). While these three—often siloed—operational units have different group priorities, report to different leadership, and work with varying budgets, they share an ultimate goal: make sure the total student population size is what it needs to be. The best tool at our disposal is to "sell" the right people the product that we most honestly have. This makes marketing, enrollment and retention monumentally easier functions. If you try to elevate the quality of the application pool via marketing or admissions versus programmatically or academically, then you are creating both an uphill battle for your marketing and admissions team, and, later, an attrition problem for Student Services on a low-to-begin-with yield.

And so, to understand your prospect's decision-making process, you must first single out (or segment) your true audience, and then map out your school's offer against their needs and wants.

The question is, how do you get to a point where you truly understand your audience? Use the proven technique, designed to humanize, in general terms, an entire segment of people: personas. If you missed the part on how to make personas, we highly encourage you to go back and read about it on page 44. Personas are a tremendous tool to become familiar with your target audience.

Case Study: Integrated Nurture

During the late fall of 2015, a highly respected private college in the Northeast region asked us to generate leads and nurture applicants to their graduate school programs. Despite a limited budget and compressed timeline, we worked quickly to develop a brand platform, creative strategy, campaign and landing page to launch shortly after the New Year.

We knew that prospects who travel to campus are more likely to convert into applicants, so we recommended that our client host an on-campus open house in April. Based on the success of previous open houses, the institution challenged us to secure 100 registrations for the event, knowing that only 40-60% of registrations would actually attend. Challenge accepted.

We worked with our client's marketing team to develop a digital media strategy that included the use of remarketing, digital radio, interstitials and banner ads on strategic digital partners in the Baltimore market, LinkedIn sponsored updates, LinkedIn InMails, and digital billboards along high traffic routes. We also facilitated a robust outreach campaign to GRE test-takers, current undergraduates, alumni and former prospects who hadn't applied to the university. We knew that combining outreach to those new to the institution with an appeal to those who knew the school well would help us both reach the right audiences and promote word-of-mouth interest.

The results were staggering. We shattered records and delivered a total of 248 open-house registrations and 125 attendees. The University's faculty and program directors were impressed enough that they went out of their way to thank our client's marketing team for delivering so many qualified prospective students. And if you've been in higher-ed marketing for a while, then you know that there's practically no higher praise than faculty approval of your work.

CONCLUSION

SO WHERE DO YOU GO FROM HERE?

We know our audience, so we know there's no easy answer for everyone who reads this book. But we can give you one piece of advice: just go do it.

Step back from the short-term goals and the politics and the performance demands. We're not saying ignore them—we also know that you certainly can't—but take the time to look at the big picture of what you're doing and then apply the OpenEDU model.

If you want to get started applying the model right away, ask yourself the following questions:

1. **What sets your institution/college/school/program apart from your competition? Why would someone choose your school over your competitors? Answering this honestly should help you define your brand platform.**

2. **What kinds of conditions and/or forces do you have to deal with? Specifically:**
   a. What's your budget?
   b. When you do you need to have your marketing program in place? In other words, what's your timeline?
   c. What are you trying to accomplish? Be as specific as possible: Awareness? Leads? Alumni participation? If you're not sure about your goal, you won't get anywhere.
   d. What's your brand? How do people feel when they come into contact with your institution/college/school/program? How do you want them to feel?

3. **Once you understand what you're up against, you need to construct the three pillars that are going to form the core of your program:**
   a. How are you going to generate traffic? What kind of traffic do you need to generate?
   b. What kind of destination are you going to create to receive the traffic that you generate? A landing page? An archived webinar? An open house? Make sure that you are clear about where the people you attract are supposed to go.
   c. Once you have a destination to capture information from the

traffic you generate, how are you going to nurture the leads you generate in order to meet your goal(s)? Email? Social media? Print mailings? Phone calls? In-person visits with candy and flowers? There's no one right way besides doing what works best for your audience(s).

4. **Finally, what's the big idea that's going to bind this entire program together? What's your strategy?** If you can't explain it in a sentence or two, it's too complicated. You should be able to articulate the reason behind what you're doing—and generally what you're going to do – in the character limit of a Tweet (140 characters or less).

We'd love to say, "See? That's all there is to it!" We really would. But we know the realities that you're probably dealing with and understand that it's a lot more complicated than just answering a few questions.

But, honestly, it doesn't have to be. While it's easy for things to get really complicated quickly, the reality is that you're trying to accomplish something while being constrained by a set of forces that are probably out of your control.

You may want to take over the world, but you've got a budget to work within, you have a timeline you have to meet, you have a goal that you're going to be evaluated on, and you've got a brand that you've got to incorporate into what you're doing.

Don't panic. This is complex stuff. But if you can define how you're going to generate **traffic** based on the audiences you're trying to reach, if you can be clear about what kind of **destination** you're going to send them to, and you have a plan to **nurture** those first tentative contacts into enrolled students, you've done what you need to do.

We're not going to say it's simple—marketing rarely is, especially higher-ed marketing—but it doesn't have to be the giant furball it so often turns into. Define objectives and stay true to them. Understand the constraints you're working under. Develop (and get consensus) on the Big Idea that's going to guide what you need to do.

Once you get that stuff in place, it's just a matter of figuring out how you're going to reach who you're after, where you're going to send them, and how you're going to move them from intention to action.

They might not care about your university now, but if you apply what you learned here, they will. We wish you all the best.

APPENDICES

APPENDIX 1: BEING A GOOD CLIENT

Over the last 20 years, our team has learned—sometimes the hard way—that relationships between clients and firms are delicate. They depend on so much. Chemistry. Honesty. Accountability. Trust. Respect. Understanding. If one element is missing, it can sabotage the others—quickly.

We're extremely lucky when it comes to client relationships. Like, play-the-lottery-now lucky. But when we unpack the strong connections we have with our clients, we find that most of them started strong. They picked us as much as we picked them. A good partner makes a good partnership. For our first lesson in Client 101, let's start with a few recommendations for picking the right agency partner. Class is in session.

The Mythology of the Perfect Partner

Imagine a leprechaun on the back of a unicorn. Now imagine that unicorn riding a dragon. Finding the perfect marketing firm may seem as mythically impossible. But there are a number of ways to weed out the hucksters and charlatans.

Hiring the right firm can change everything for your institution. Hiring the wrong one can be a disaster. Never mind the loss of internal credibility you'll be saddled with for picking the wrong firm: A truly bad fit can result in the loss of time, money, brand equity and gains your competitors will make while you wrestle to make a failed relationship work.

Dealing with a failed relationship can be paralyzing on its own, but it's not like the world stops while you fix your problem: you still have deadlines to meet, goals to accomplish and bosses to please.

We get it. Hiring a marketing firm can be scary. But it doesn't have to be an exercise in nail biting. Here are six golden rules to help you find that not-so-mythical right fit.

1. **Be honest.** If your institutional culture is "fast and furious," be demanding; if the pace is more gradual, drag your feet. See how a potential partner responds. Can they match your pace? Do

they get frustrated? Do they seem to understand? If they are going take issue with how you work before they land your work, they're going to be downright toxic after you hire them.

2. **Share the risk.** Everyone knows that there is risk associated with signing a marketing firm. What if they are terrible to work with? What if they're not responsive? What if they're a bunch of prima donnas who can't take direction? What if they just don't "get" you?

   You might not realize that they're also taking a risk signing on with you. What if you want 24-7 service? What if you don't like any of the work and are unable to communicate clearly why? What if you're a monster? What if your funding dries up? Acknowledging that there is risk for both parties and openly talking about it should stimulate an honest discussion that can serve as the framework for mitigating some of that risk… together.

3. **Ask tough questions.** Nelson Mandela once said, "No one truly knows a nation until one has been inside its jails. A nation should not be judged by how it treats its highest citizens, but its lowest ones." It's easy to be awesome when things are awesome, but how will the firm behave when the wheels come spinning off? Give them a tough scenario and ask them how they'd handle it. Insist on specifics.

4. **Ask to meet the team—the REAL team.** Agencies are notorious for sending their "A team" of slick sales people and top talent to pitches. Who can blame them? They need to make an airtight case for you to hire them. You're not going to land many accounts with a junior-junior copywriter and a social media coordinator whose college ID hasn't expired yet.

   Not surprisingly, clients take the bait. They award the work to the A-team. And far too often, they'll never see those people again. The school's marketing team is astonished when they sit down to that first kickoff meeting after the contract is signed, only to find the B-team: lower-level staff who can count their years of experience on their fingers and still have plenty of hand left.

5. **Try, then buy.** If you have the time and money, hire two or three firms for short, one-off projects. Something small and

quick. If you really want to push it, give them the option to pick between two small projects such as one that appeals to emotion or another that requires a more rational, data-driven approach. Note which one they pick. Give them a tight deadline and pay careful attention to what questions they ask and what they deliver.

Some firms you encounter may choose to exclude themselves from the exercise. That's a good thing. If they don't have the foresight to see this as an opportunity to "test drive" the relationship, how interested could they be in working with you in the first place?

6. **Don't let yourself be fascinated.** There have been many books written on how to pitch well. Savvy marketers practice techniques to make you feel intrigued, dazzled, happy, excited, and hopeful. Their job is to enchant people, whether it's consumers or your marketing team. This is not to say great presenters can't follow through with a great relationship and great work. They can.

   But fight the urge to give the work to the shiniest firm (it can be tough, we know)—give the work to the most qualified company.

7. **Remember that great pitchers don't always make great partners.** Sure, a great argument can be made that firms that present well will also know best how to sell your products and services. But often, as you peel the proverbial onion, you'll get closer to the truth… and it could involve tears. We submit three truths:

   - The bigger the firm, the less likely the folks that pulled on our heartstrings will work on your account.
   - Unless the delightful people pitching the heck out of you are going to literally take their show on the road, they aren't going to be the ones selling your products and/or services. Their ads are. Know the difference.
   - Most of the techniques and characteristics that generate a strong emotional appeal in person don't transfer all that well to a mass communication medium. Expert presenters use a host of verbal and nonverbal techniques to get you to feel what they

want you to feel. Don't let yourself get wrapped up. Weigh both the proposal (rational) and the presentation (emotional) as equal parts of the equation and make the best selection based on all the data, not just the presentation.

Who knows, maybe there are leprechauns-riding-unicorns-riding-dragons out there, but in absence of concrete evidence, do yourself a favor: Pick the best partner for you based on all the evidence, not just how you feel after the pitch.

Working with An Agency

Of course, once you hire an agency, you have to actually work with them. Most of the time, it takes months upon months to select a partner. And by that time, you are probably behind on your recruitment cycle and things need to move fast. Hopefully you chose wisely, but regardless, and like it or not, you are most likely stuck with this partner for at least a year. So, the question is: how can you structure the relationship to work successfully?

At the root of every good relationship is respect. Respect is a funny thing because that's not the type of thing you can just ask for or simply give. Respect is earned. And it's earned over time. Until you've had enough time and experience with the new partner, there are a few things that you can do every day to be respectful.

For example, you can be respectful with their time by making the most out of meetings. Make sure your team is organized and prepared before calls or meetings. Insist on an agenda either from the agency or your team, depending on whose responsibility it is, and understand that chaos on your end eats up budget and weakens results.

Marketing is a team sport. There is no reasonable expectation that an agency will ever know the ins and outs of your organization as intimately as you do. An honest agency will know and embrace this.

A good client will also understand that the one or two projects they are working on is just one or two projects of tens—or maybe even hundreds—that the agency will work on each year. Agencies might not know all of your particular ins and outs, but they should have considerable experience running similar projects.

This mutual understanding can serve as tremendous platform for collaboration and leverage. It can be scary to acknowledge that you don't know something or that you don't have as much experience, but the most successful relationships are the ones where honesty rules. Be o.k. with not knowing everything and give both yourself and your agency permission to ask for help to watch the relationship bloom.

Along the same lines, if you have data or insight that could help the agency do a better job for you, give it to them. And do so regularly and in a timely fashion. Generating primary data takes time and effort. If you've got some already, help advance your own outcomes by sharing it with your agency.

Honesty goes a long way in all relationships. But don't misunderstand being honest with being mean. Try, as hard as it might sometimes be, to assume the best and confirm the worst.

There is nothing like that ineffable feeling you get when you know you jumped the gun by unjustly accusing someone of something. Taking back bad energy is a lot harder to do than just assuming the best and confirming the worst. And while being honest doesn't need to be mean, it should be blunt.

No one has time for beating around the bush and, as it happens, agencies have thick skins. If something's not working, be upfront and clear about it. Don't wait for things to go downhill. At the first sign of a problem, nip it.

Also, much like good parents, fighting in front of the kids is never a good idea. Don't put agencies in the middle of internal disagreements. You'll probably be on the clock through it all, and the more time they spend as counselors, the less time they have to do research and creative work for you.

Along the same lines, don't ask agencies to take sides. They should remain objective and be guided by what makes the most sense for the institution. If you allow them to keep an independent position, then they'll have broader credibility when they take on other issues that impact the institution.

Finally, define and communicate your expectations for excellence. If you're providing regular feedback and measurements, everyone's on the same page. Be clear, reasonable, and fair about the items agencies should deliver. Ambiguous targets are hard, if not impossible hit. Give your agency a fighting chance to be a good partner.

APPENDIX 2: RESEARCH RESOURCES

During the creation of this book, we amassed a catalog of helpful websites. Instead of including the entire list, we've decided to focus on our favorites. Segmented by theme, these compelling sites provide creative inspiration, germane content, and a jolt to spark innovative minds.

Advertising Websites

SmartBrief is a leading digital B2B media company. By combining technology and editorial expertise, SmartBrief delivers each day's most relevant industry news to more than 5.8 million senior executives, thought leaders and informed industry professionals.

Seth Godin's blog riffs on marketing, respect, and the ways ideas spread.

The Donut websites are aimed at helping businesses to succeed by providing reliable information and resources that can save business owners time and money. With an engaging mix of how-to guides, feature articles, checklists, expert Q&A's, FAQs, case studies, video content and blogs, each site provides new and established businesses with free advice about how to manage a range of key tasks and issues.

Business Websites

Bloomberg Business delivers business and markets news, data, analysis, and video to the world, featuring stories from *Business Week* and Bloomberg News.

Harvard Business Publishing (HBP) was founded in 1994 as a not-for-profit, wholly owned subsidiary of Harvard University that reports into Harvard Business School. Their mission is to improve the practice of management in a changing world, which influences how we approach what we do here and what we believe is important. Harvard Business Publishing serves as a bridge between academia and enterprises around the globe through its publications and multiple platforms for content delivery, and its reach into three markets: academic, corporate, and individual managers.

The publisher of *Inc.* Magazine, inc.com is the perfect resource where you can find everything you need to know to start and grow your business. Get advice, tools, and services that help your small business grow.

Culture Websites

Cool Hunting is an award-winning publication that uncovers the latest in design, technology, style, travel, art and culture. This talented team of writers, editors, videographers, designers and developers publish original content that has informed the creative community since 2003.

Flavorwire is a publication of Flavorpill Media, a network of culturally connected people, covering events, art, books, music, film, TV, and pop culture the world over. Flavorwire features global cultural news and commentary, original reporting, and the occasional cat photo (this is the Internet, after all).

The Verge covers the intersection of technology, science, art, and culture. This publication offers in-depth reporting and long-form feature stories, breaking news coverage, product information, and community content in a unified and cohesive manner.

Websites

Daily dot is the ultimate destination for the latest news, opinions and in-depth reporting from around the Internet. No wonder it's known as the hometown newspaper of the World Wide Web.

Contently is a technology company that helps brands create great content at scale. They provide companies technology, content marketing expertise, and creative – journalists, photographers, designers, videographers, etc.

ClickZ is the largest resource of interactive marketing news, information, commentary, advice, opinion, research, and reference in the world, online or off. From search to social, technology to trends, their coverage is expert, exclusive, and in-depth and supports their mission to help interactive marketers do their jobs better.

Education Websites

Educational Technology and Mobile Learning is operated by a team of dedicated teachers located in Canada and serves as a resource of education web tools and mobile apps for teachers and educators

The Atlantic Education is a subdivision of news and opinions about higher education from top thinkers.

University Business is the most widely received and regularly read publication for higher education leaders at two-and four-year colleges and universities nationwide. UB provides cutting-edge coverage of higher education technology, news, finance, policy, profiles and more to this exclusive audience across print, digital and in-person event platform.

Reading List

Client, friends and conference attendees often ask us to share our reading list. We also noted that The Model was built using spare parts from researchers and strategists who came before us. It only makes sense to honor and credit the most influential of the lot here. As with everything in life, there are things about each book that we will fight to the end for and things we reject outright. It's all part of the process, we imagine, but we encourage you to do the same with our books and the books listed here. Enjoy.

Think Like a Freak: The Authors of Freakonomics Offer to Retrain Your Brain,
Steven D. Levitt and Stephen J. Dubner; William Morrow Paperbacks, 2014.

This book encourages you to think against the grain. To think like a child. To ask "why?" And to avoid conventional wisdom. We like this book because it gives us techniques for critical thinking and "break the guessing machine" (see Made to Stick). Coincidentally, this might be a good primer for people interested in the foundations of "Design Thinking."

Fascinate: Your 7 Triggers to Persuasion and Captivation,
Sally Hogshead; Harper Business, 2010.

We saw Sally present the principles of Fascinate at xyx conference. This book is chock-full of very powerful stuff that, when applied properly, can be used for persuasion. The seven triggers are: Innovation, Passion, Power, Prestige, Trust, Mystique and Alert. Each trigger has its own strategic scaffolding and we can see entire books written on every one. We like this book because it offers a tactical model for brand positioning and even campaign strategy.

Switch: How to Change Things When Change Is Hard,
Chip Heath and Dan Heath; Random House, 2010.

This book uses a simple metaphor to help us understand how to get people to switch or change their behavior: imagine a person riding and guiding an elephant along a path. The Rider represents reason, the Elephant represents emotion and the Path represents the context in which the desired outcome exists. The basic premise of the book is that change is hard. No one wants to do it, but if you can skillfully direct the Rider, motivate the Elephant and shape the Path you might actually be in a position to effect change.

Made to Stick: Why Some Ideas Survive and Others Die,
Chip Heath and Dan Heath; Random House, 2006.

The authors outline a framework that copywriters, marketers and advertisers can follow to make their messages stickier. If this book reminds of you Malcolm Gladwell's *Tipping Point,* it is because they are very similar in style and content. The Heath brothers draw from psychosocial studies on memory, emotion and motivation to help us craft and position messages that stay with people.

Contagious: Why Things Catch On,
Jonah Berger; Simon & Schuster, 2013.

Berger suggests the six rules that govern how content becomes viral, or contagious. The principles are rooted in memory, psychology, economics, and sociology. Since many books on our list reference some of the same studies, what you read here may start to sound familiar. We like this book because it structures already familiar concepts and studies to help us craft messages that are not only sticky and effective, but also viral.

Buyology: Truth and Lies About Why We Buy,
Martin Lindstrom; Currency, 2008.

This is a fast read about how and why we make "buy" decisions. The insights germinate from an impressive, three-year global Neuromarketing study. If you can get past the author's runaway ego, and focus squarely on the content, you'll get a lot out of this book. And, as with all great power (that you will have after reading this book), comes great responsibility.

Brainfluence: 100 Ways to Persuade and Convince Consumers with Neuromarketing,
Roger Dooley; John Wiley & Sons, 2011.

Another good book on Neuromarketing. This one is very tactical, however. For example, did you know a red button drives more action? Over 20% more action. And that's just one of 99 other neuromarketing-based tips you can find in this book.

The 22 Immutable Laws of Branding,
Al Ries and Laura Ries; Harper Business, 1998.

There are few books this pointed and useful about branding. Al and Laura Ries methodically outline the 22 laws of branding. We imagine that the chances of there being exactly 22 laws are very slim. If we had to guess, they chose the number "22" to key-off their first book, *The 22 Immutable Laws of Marketing*—which ironically, contradicts immutable branding law *14: The Law of Sub-brands.* They argue, "What branding builds, sub-branding can destroy." Just the same, it's a great book and don't let our persnicketness rob you from solid fundamentals.

The Laws of Simplicity (Simplicity: Design, Technology, Business, Life),
John Maeda; MIT Press, 2006.

Even though this book should have been about fifty pages shorter (keeping with the spirit of the book's title), it does offer a number of models that will help you design with simplicity. The author outlines the three laws of simplicity: reduce, organize and time. It's a tremendous read and we think you'll get a lot out of it.

Present Shock: When Everything Happens Now,
Douglas Rushkoff; Riverhead Books, 2008.

Conversation is a dying art form. When people chat and a question comes up that nobody has the answer to, debate, exploration, or critical thinking does not ensue. Someone whips out a mobile phone and Googles the answer. And just like that, the topic, the inquiry, the intellectual growth opportunity is dead on the spot. There is a generation in the making that is very good at answering questions. But no one commits any of it to memory. That makes it more difficult to connect the dots and think critically. We like this book because it dives into technology and its impact on culture, knowledge and memory.

Drive: The Surprising Truth About What Motivates Us,
Daniel H. Pink; Riverhead Books, 2008.

Have you ever wondered how to motivate creative types? It's not necessarily always money. Did you know timesheets were an artifact of the industrial revolution? And yet we still use it to measure productivity – meanwhile, we are thinking about our work in the car, at dinner, in the shower. What's more, most creative breakthroughs don't happen while on the clock. So, how do you motivate creative people? This book has a lot to say about that.

David and Goliath: Underdogs, Misfits, and the Art of Battling Giants,
Malcolm Gladwell; Little, Brown and Company, 2011.

From the very beginning, Gladwell captivates readers by retelling an adage story through different lens. As it turns out, it wasn't a miracle that David beat Goliath. It just seems like it would have been because he was small and Goliath was big. But David brought a "gun" to a knife fight. Back then, David and other experienced slingers could projectile a rock with at the stopping power of a .45mm handgun with high accuracy from up to 200 yards away. Goliath didn't have a chance. This book is about how the little guys, more often than not, have the advantage.